ESL/ELL TEACHER'S GUIDE

PACEMAKER®

Economics

GLOBE FEARON
Pearson Learning Group

Pacemaker® Economics, Third Edition

We would like to thank the following educators, who provided valuable comments and suggestions during the development of this book.

Reviewers

Ann Hilborn, former ESL/ELL teacher, coordinator, and curriculum writer for the Houston Independent School District; currently an ESL/ELL consultant in Texas

Elizabeth Jimenez, GEMAS Consulting, Pomona, CA

Project Staff

Art and Design: Evelyn Bauer, Joan Jacobus, Jennifer Visco
Editorial: Stephanie Cahill, Jane Petlinski, Jennie Rakos, Shirley White
Manufacturing: Thomas Dunne
Marketing: Katie Erezuma, Douglas Falk
Production: Irene Belinsky, Louis Campos, Jill Kuhfuss, Cynthia Lynch
Publishing Operations: Carolyn Coyle, Tom Daning, Richetta Lobban
Technology: Joanne Saito

All photography © Pearson Education, Inc. (PEI) unless otherwise specifically noted.

Cover: *bkgd.* Steve Cole/PhotoDisc, Inc.; *l.* Robert George Young/Masterfile; *m.r.* Sandra Baker/Stone/Getty Images; *b.r.* Russ Lappa/Prentice Hall School.

ISBN 0-13-024370-1
Printed in the United States of America
1 2 3 4 5 6 7 8 9 10   08 07 06 05 04 03

Globe Fearon
Pearson Learning Group

1-800-321-3106
www.pearsonlearning.com

Contents

Teaching ESL/ELL Students in the Classroom

As cross-cultural mobility increases, teachers are mindful of their responsibility in the preparation of global citizens. All classrooms are becoming ESL/ELL classrooms, and many teachers are confronting new instructional challenges as demographics shift and diversity multiplies.

On the one hand, there is concern for meeting the needs of students who bring issues and challenges that teachers often feel underprepared to meet. On the other, there is renewal and excitement as teachers and students open to the perspectives of other cultures, and classrooms assume an international orientation.

Helping the ESL/ELL student to succeed in the academic classroom has required all educators to rethink their role as teacher, to search for new instructional tools, and to become simultaneously a language teacher, reading teacher, and academic content teacher. To help teachers meet this formidable task, both students and teachers must have teaching and learning resources that make academic content accessible.

The Pacemaker® Curriculum

Typically, schools adopt one of two structures for academic classes: sheltered content or regular mainstream. The Pacemaker® curriculum is perfectly suited for either of those environments. Designed for students who read independently at a 3.0 to 4.0 reading level, a Pacemaker® text normally corresponds to a student at the mid-intermediate level of language proficiency. This level is the one at which most ESL/ELL students are required to be in order to deal with the cognitively demanding language of academic content classes.

Because the Pacemaker® materials are within the expected reading levels of a second-language learner and the content is presented in manageable sections, ESL/ELL students are encouraged and enabled to be active participants rather than silent observers in the academic classroom.

When students are given sheltered content instruction, the Pacemaker® curriculum is an ideal classroom text for intermediate and advanced level students. In schools where sheltered content classes are unavailable, Pacemaker® can be a valuable text or resource for ESL/ELL students in the regular content classroom because it provides information in small manageable sections at a level that students can comprehend.

When Pacemaker® materials are provided in place of, or in addition to, the standard text, students can access academic content rather than struggle with a grade-level text that is beyond their current language proficiency. Although the language skills of ESL/ELL students are in a developmental stage, they can be held to the same high standards of critical inquiry as their on-level classmates when input is comprehensible. The Pacemaker® curriculum is also an ideal tool that can be used to prepare students for their grade-level tests.

How Do I Use the *Pacemaker® Economics ESL/ELL Teacher's Guide?*

Teaching academic content requires attention to both information and skills. Although content teachers are not reading teachers, time spent previewing and engaging in prestudy activities provides an opportunity to teach valuable skills that will serve students in all areas of studies. For ESL/ELL students, time spent in previewing will assure greater comprehension and retention. It will prepare them not only for reading, but also for participation in class discussions, collaborative work, and individual or group projects.

The suggestions on the following pages are easily managed in a sheltered content class. If the class is a regular content class, ESL/ELL students can be provided with a Pacemaker® text while others use a grade-level text. If an aide is not available to work with ESL/ELL students and the teacher works with both groups, it is not necessary to divide the class and teach two separate groups. Using the high-interest Pacemaker® texts for ESL/ELL students makes it possible to integrate two different texts under unifying objectives. The abundance of resources in the Pacemaker® curriculum to support instruction makes it possible to provide alternate materials with minimum effort.

Each chapter of the *Pacemaker® Economics* Student Edition is supported by a two-page lesson plan, which follows an Into-Through-Beyond model. The lesson plan begins by introducing students to the chapter content, or bringing them into the content. It then helps students to work through the content they have acquired by engaging in relevant activities. Finally, it takes students beyond what they have learned by assessing what they learned and affording them an opportunity to summarize the important points of the chapter.

▶ Introducing the Chapter

This section is made up of two parts: Tapping Prior Knowledge and Preteaching Vocabulary.

Tapping Prior Knowledge

All students, ESL/ELL students in particular, improve comprehension when they can connect what they already know to the subject. Focusing on the colorful artwork, the title, a caption, a subheading, or a Pacemaker® feature will help students to make important initial connections.

Tapping Prior Knowledge gives students the opportunity to

- Preview the chapter
- Access their prior knowledge about a topic
- Think about an overarching question that connects students' prior knowledge to chapter content

Preteaching Vocabulary

Preteaching Vocabulary offers students an opportunity to

- Identify and define words and phrases that are unfamiliar to them. You may wish to ask students to keep a Word Log in which they can list the words and phrases that they identify for Personalizing Vocabulary. This activity is also an opportunity for students to learn the proper pronunciation of the vocabulary words and phrases. When reviewing pronunciation, you may wish to use one of the following approaches: pronounce the words and have students listen to the pronunciation, pronounce the words and ask students to repeat each one, or pronounce the words and have students repeat them in a choral read.

- Engage in a variety of activities across chapters that are based on specific, academic content words and phrases that are integral to students' understanding of the subject matter as well as words and phrases that are challenging for ESL/ELL students, such as double-meaning words and phrases and idiomatic expressions.

- Use the vocabulary strategies discussed on page xiii of this guide.

▶ Learning Objectives

All learners need concrete and concise explanations of what they will be expected to learn. Every Pacemaker® outlines specific Learning Objectives for each chapter. Reading those objectives with your students as they begin the chapter connects them all to the same goals, guides the lesson, and helps to prepare students for future assessment.

Turn to the end of the chapter and have students work in pairs or small groups to connect the Learning Objectives to the Chapter Review. Make sure that students use the questions in the text to guide them in reading and understanding. ESL/ELL students need to be directed to these tools and shown how the tools can help them to understand what they are reading and studying. Using these tools will also reinforce what students are expected to learn. You may wish to distribute copies of the Chapter Goals and Self-Assessment found on page 67 of this guide and have students write the list of objectives that they are expected to master by the end of the chapter. Completing this sheet will allow students to evaluate their own achievement of learning goals.

▶ Applying Content Knowledge

All students improve comprehension when they are able to apply what they have learned. Activities that incorporate the use of graphic organizers as well as activities that allow students to (re)address chapter content help cultivate the initial connections they made in Tapping Prior Knowledge.

Each activity in Applying Content Knowledge

- Uses Specifically Designed Academic Instruction in English strategies. SDAIE strategies focus on delivering grade-level content and covering grade-level standards in a way that is relevant for and comprehensible to the student.

- Uses the Cognitive Academic Language Learning Approach. CALLA is designed to help ESL/ELL students succeed academically by addressing topics from the major content subjects, developing academic language skills, and offering explicit instruction on learning strategies.
- Offers activities that enhance students' content knowledge through reading, writing, speaking, and listening.
- Allows students to use a variety of graphic organizers. Several organizers are provided on pages 50–63 of this guide. Using them will not only help students to understand what they read, it will also teach them the variety of ways material can be organized.

▶ Assessing Content Knowledge

This section provides three levels of questions tailored to beginning level ESL/ELL students, intermediate level ESL/ELL students, and advanced level ESL/ELL students. (See page viii of this guide for placement criteria.) Questions can be answered orally or in writing. This section also provides teachers' annotations at point of use.

As an alternative, the leveled questions can also be used for discussion. If the questions are used for discussion, allow ESL/ELL students adequate time to process the questions by using a cooperative strategy, such as putting students in small groups made up of students with varied language abilities. Pose the question and then allow the group to process the answer so that each group member can respond. Then, allow one member of each group to give an answer. This strategy is also ideal for reviewing chapter content.

Beginning Level Students

- Specific page references are provided to scaffold beginning level ESL/ELL students.
- Beginning level ESL/ELL students are asked to respond to questions by using short verbal responses.

Intermediate Level Students

- Specific page references are provided to scaffold intermediate level ESL/ELL students.
- Intermediate level ESL/ELL students are asked to respond to questions by using verbal responses or short written responses.

Advanced Level Students

- Because advanced students are expected to be able to answer the questions in the Chapter Review at the end of each chapter in the Student Edition, no page references are provided for the advanced level ESL/ELL students.
- Advanced level ESL/ELL students are asked to respond to questions in complete written sentences.

▶ Closing the Chapter

Closing the Chapter provides an opportunity for students to assess the key points of the chapter and to summarize them. Students are frequently asked to write a summary or complete a graphic organizer about what they learned, but you may wish to ask beginning level ESL/ELL students to give an oral report of what they learned.

Selecting the Appropriate Leveled Questions

This guide includes three levels of questions to address the different levels of students' language proficiency.

Because there are students who can speak English but have difficulty reading it, the leveled questions presented in this guide should be chosen for a student based on the student's level of reading proficiency. The following criteria are based on student competencies at the beginning of the year. The three levels of questions provided in each lesson plan of this guide are also available as reproducible pages that can be downloaded from www.esl-ell.com. Level A corresponds to the Beginning Level Questions; Level B corresponds to the Intermediate Level Questions; and Level C corresponds to the Advanced Level Questions.

▶ Beginning Level Questions – Level A

Beginning Level Students

- Range from having no reading comprehension to being able to read and comprehend simple sentences in present continuous or simple present tense
- Are able to answer straightforward comprehension questions (*who, what, when, where*) that require only simple responses
- Are able to write paragraphs of one to five lines
- Are able to read and write at a kindergarten or a first-grade level
- Should be able to complete the Beginning Level Questions in this guide

▶ Intermediate Level Questions – Level B

Intermediate Level Students

- Satisfy all of the beginning level criteria
- Are able to read and comprehend simple past and future tense sentences
- Are able to answer comprehension questions that also include *how* and *why* with more complex responses
- Are able to write a well-developed paragraph
- Are able to read and write from a second- to a fourth-grade level
- Should be able to complete the Intermediate Level Questions in this guide

▶ Advanced Level Questions – Level C

Advanced Level Students

- Satisfy all of the beginning and intermediate level criteria
- Are able to read and comprehend more complex sentence constructions
- Are able to use past and some perfect tense constructions in their writing
- Are able to respond to questions that require inference and conclusions
- Are able to write multiparagraph compositions
- Are able to read and write at a level that can extend from third to fifth grade
- Should be able to complete the questions in the Chapter Review in the Student Edition as well as the Advanced Level Questions in this guide

General Strategies for ESL/ELL Students

Although the *Pacemaker® Economics ESL/ELL Teacher's Guide* is designed to assist teachers of ESL/ELL students to help their students access content knowledge, there are some additional strategies that are centered around motivating ESL/ELL students and promoting effective study skills.

▶ Classroom Techniques

Encourage risk taking by maintaining a low-anxiety environment.

- Strive for genuine communication with students. Students' fears are calmed when teachers share information about themselves and invite students to talk about themselves and their experiences.
- Provide game-like activities.
- Adjust speech. Speak a little more slowly and distinctly.
- Share information across cultures.
- Provide materials that support comprehension.
- Practice the students' languages.

Provide academic scaffolds to help your students access the content.

- Model all activities for your students. Provide examples and writing models.
- Give students a topic outline for note taking.
- Encourage students to use previewing strategies, while-reading strategies, and postreading strategies.
- Provide study questions and guides.
- Identify organizational cues, such as headings, subheadings, and charts.
- Afford students longer reading time as well as extended time for assignments and test completion.

▶ Building Language Skills

Read to students. By reading short passages in answer to a question or as an introduction, ESL/ELL students receive the added benefit of hearing academic language, cadence, rhythm, and pronunciation.

When reading from a source other than the Student Edition, provide handouts or use an overhead so that students can see and hear the information.

Teach students to read academic material several times. As academic learners, we all expect to read a selection, a page, a chapter, or a section more than once. Encourage students to

- Survey an academic assignment once for general information and vocabulary
- Organize reading into smaller chunks for understanding
- Read a third time for higher-level critical-thinking skills

In-class reading time is usually no more than 10 to 15 minutes. Regular classroom students may be expected to read more material in that time frame, but they need not read for a longer period of time. (A more detailed discussion of previewing strategies is presented on page xii of this guide.)

Maximize language output. Although students should be given opportunities to interact without depending heavily on language, the more practical opportunities students have to speak and write, the more proficient they will become. These opportunities may begin with communication of their own life experiences and world knowledge.

Provide open-ended writing assignments and opportunities for ESL/ELL students to express their thoughts and feelings. Some of these include

- Journals
- Descriptions of experiences or feelings
- Responses to art, photographs, and audiovisuals

The Tapping Prior Knowledge section, which often asks students to relate the content to their own experiences, is an ideal opportunity for students to express their thoughts and feelings. For example, you may wish to ask students to keep a journal and record their initial responses to the visual image(s) that appear(s) on the first page of each chapter. You may also consider having students choose a visual image that appears in the chapter.

Complete activities with a writing assignment. ESL/ELL students may need adjustments to the writing assignments, such as

- Shorter writing assignments
- More time to complete writing
- Frequent opportunities to work with peers in revising and editing

Occasionally, it will be necessary to assign a different topic. The *Pacemaker® Economics ESL/ELL Teacher's Guide* provides writing opportunities in conjunction with many of the activities that help students reinforce chapter content.

▶ Learning Strategies

Provide opportunities for groups to work together, share information, and be a resource for each other.

Provide opportunities for students to interact without depending heavily on language. Students can work to access content knowledge by

- Doing projects and making posters, pictures, and collages
- Using manipulatives
- Using charts
- Using numbered lists, bulleted lists, graphs, tables, and models
- Role-playing

Use visuals, pictures, realia, video clips, and actions to teach vocabulary and to make concepts concrete and understandable. Maps, play money, artwork, globes, and pictures are effective, tangible ways to help students access content.

Use graphic organizers for note taking, organizing information, and writing. Diagrams and charts are effective ways to teach students to organize information and visualize patterns and structures. Graphic organizers can be downloaded from www.esl-ell.com.

▶ Customizing Student Assessment

Assess your students' successes by focusing on the "big picture."

- Evaluate both process and product.
- Recognize effort and improvement in ways other than grades.
- Allow rewrites and test corrections to improve grades and understanding.
- Congratulate students on small successes.
- Focus on meaning and content knowledge, not grammar mistakes, in students' written work.
- Use alternative assessments such as performance-based assessments, self-ratings, projects, and portfolios.
- Adjust your grading scale when appropriate.

▶ At Home

Help students manage their own success. Reinforce the importance of organizing homework, academic tasks, and extracurricular activities using a schedule like the one shown below.

Monday	Tuesday	Wednesday	Thursday	Friday
Soccer practice 3:00–5:30	Study time 5:00–6:00	Soccer practice 3:00–5:30	Study time 5:00–6:00	
Dinner 6:00–7:00	Dinner 6:00–7:00	Dinner 6:00–7:00	Dinner 6:00–7:00	Dinner 6:00–7:00
Study time 7:00–8:00	Orchestra 7:30–9:00		Climbing club 8:00–9:00	

You may wish to work with students to schedule activities from this guide that you assign as homework. Homework gives families an opportunity to become involved with their children.

Ann Hilborn

Ann Hilborn, a former ESL/ELL teacher, coordinator, and curriculum writer for the Houston Independent School District, is currently an ESL/ELL consultant in Texas.

Previewing Strategies for ESL/ELL Students

When students preview, they set a purpose for reading, think about what they already know about a topic, and get a general idea of what they will learn. Activities that students engage in before reading help them prepare to learn new information. Previewing helps students incorporate what they read into their existing knowledge. During previewing, students should identify key terms, assess the level of difficulty and length of what they will be reading, gain a general sense of the topic and major subtopics, understand text organization, and determine how this information relates to what they already know.

▶ Create a Plan for Reading.

This task requires students to think about why they are reading. *What was the purpose of the assignment?* If students are unclear about the answer to this question, they need to find out why they are reading. Next, students should look at the assignment to get a sense of how difficult it is. *Can they read the assignment in one session or should they break it into several sessions?*

▶ Think About What They Know About the Topic.

Students who engage with the text create a scaffold for learning. When they bring prior knowledge to bear on their readings, students become involved with the text.

▶ Preview the Selection.

When students preview, they think about what they already know about a topic and get a general idea of what they will learn. Students should

- Look at the title and subheadings. They usually signal important ideas and hint at text organization.

- Look at other visual aids. These aids include words within the text in italic or boldface type, which may be vocabulary words or new concepts. Students should also look at maps, photographs, charts, illustrations, numbered lists, and bulleted lists. These visuals will give ESL/ELL students more contextual information to aid with comprehension.

- Read the first and last paragraphs. These paragraphs often contain the thesis or major points of the reading. Remind students to connect what they are previewing with what they already know about the topic.

- Read the first sentence or topic sentence of each paragraph. Often, the main point of a paragraph is found at the beginning.

- Get an idea of the text structure. If students understand how the text is organized—for example, chronologically or in cause-and-effect form—they will be better able to follow the text.

Vocabulary Strategies for ESL/ELL Students

Each two-page lesson plan provides a vocabulary activity for its chapter. Although the vocabulary activities in this guide support the chapters in which they are featured, they can also be used for any other chapter in the book. In addition to the specific vocabulary activities offered in this guide, the following items are some general vocabulary strategies to consider when teaching new vocabulary to students.

▶ Create Word Logs.

Encourage students to keep Word Logs that they can use to record the vocabulary they identify for the Personalizing Vocabulary activity. The Word Log can be a spiral notebook divided by letters of the alphabet, with a second section for phrases. Students can write definitions, sentences, or draw or cut pictures from magazines to aid in their understanding and remembering.

▶ Pronounce Vocabulary Words and Phrases.

It is critical to pronounce vocabulary words and phrases. As in the case of reading aloud to your students, pronouncing new words and phrases allows students to grow accustomed to cadence and rhythm. When reviewing pronunciation of vocabulary words and phrases, you may wish to

- Pronounce each word and phrase and have students listen to the pronunciation
- Pronounce each word and phrase and ask students to repeat each one
- Pronounce each word and phrase and then have students repeat them in a choral read
- Provide a phonetic respelling for students to use in addition to the strategies mentioned above

▶ Think About the Topic.

Help students make a connection between the new vocabulary word or phrase and a word or phrase in their own language. This strategy allows them to see the word or phrase in their native language and aids retention. Suggest also that ESL/ELL students refer to their first language for cognates or similar words.

▶ Monitor Comprehension.

Students have several opportunities to learn the academic vocabulary that appears in the Student Edition. However, students are not always comfortable or familiar with all of the words and phrases used in daily conversation, such as idiomatic expressions and colloquialisms. Ask students if they understand the words and phrases that you use during the course of your lesson delivery. Your inquiry can be after a few sentences or after the use of a word or expression that you are unsure your students understand, but it should be frequent.

What Is Economics? pages 2–15

▶ Introducing the Chapter

Tapping Prior Knowledge

Ask students what they would do if they were given a certain amount of money. Would they spend the money on things that they need, things that they do not need but would like to have, or save the money? Inform students that economics is the study of how people, businesses, and nations make choices. Some of these choices are how to spend money. Ask students to suggest reasons why knowledge of economics is important.

Preteaching Vocabulary

Personalizing Vocabulary Begin by asking students to preview the chapter for five unfamiliar words or phrases and to record them in their Word Logs. Ask students to use their bilingual dictionaries to define the words or phrases.

Identifying Essential Vocabulary Go over the pronunciation and meaning of each word or phrase in the box below. Next, distribute an index card to each student. Ask students to write a question on the index card using one or more of the vocabulary terms. Then, have students exchange cards with a partner and answer their partner's question.

Word or Phrase	Meaning
tuck the money away	not spend the money (p. 4)
torn	not able to decide (p. 4)
a fact of life	something that cannot be changed (p. 4)
meet their needs	get what they need (p. 5)
animated film	a film made by photographing a series of drawings so that the figures in them seem to move (p. 7)
a trade-off	a compromise (p. 8)
research and development	inventing and making new products (p.13)

▶ Applying Content Knowledge

From the Chapter: Photographs (pages 5 and 7)

Have students compare the photographs of workplaces found on pages 5 and 7 of the Student Edition. Prompt students to discuss the differences in both workplaces with questions such as *What kinds of goods are for sale in the photograph of the electronics store? What services might the workers provide in the office on page 7?* Then, have students identify other examples of workers providing goods and services in photographs in magazines. Allow time for students to exhibit and discuss the photographs they find.

Organizing Information

Distribute copies of the KWL Chart found on page 59 of this guide. Before you begin to study the chapter, allow students to complete the **K** and the **W** columns of the chart. Ask students, *What would you like to learn in this chapter?* Have students complete the **L** column of the chart once they have completed the chapter.

Personalizing the Lesson

Distribute copies of the Spider Web found on page 54 of this guide. Ask students to label the topic heading **Factors of Production**. In each corner of the web, have students identify and label the four factors of production: **Entrepreneurs**, **Natural Resources**, **Labor**, and **Capital**. Next, have students form pairs. Have pairs suppose that they are entrepreneurs and have them fill in their own names under that category. Ask pairs what new goods or services they would like to make or provide. Then, have them list the other factors of production that they might need to make their new business idea successful. You may want to provide some examples for students.

Assessing Content Knowledge

Ask students to respond to the following questions. You may wish to encourage students with higher language proficiency to help beginning level students understand the questions.

Beginning Level Questions

Encourage students at this level to think about the answers to these questions and to offer short verbal responses.

1. Look at page 4. Does *scarcity* mean we have too much or not enough of something? (not enough)

2. Look at page 5. Are needs or wants the things we must have to survive? (needs)

3. Read page 6. What are two factors of production? (Possible answers: natural resources, labor, capital, entrepreneurs)

4. Read the last paragraph on page 9. True or false: Opportunity costs occur any time that a choice is made. (true)

5. Find the word *technology* on page 11. What meaning is given for it? (science at work)

Intermediate Level Questions

Encourage students at this level to offer verbal responses or short written responses to the following questions.

1. Look at page 3. What is the study of how people, businesses, and governments choose to use their limited resources called? (economics)

2. Look at the photograph on page 5. What are some goods that this store sells? (Possible answers: telephones, answering machines, fax machines, copiers)

3. Look at the photograph on page 7. What factor of production is shown in the photograph? (labor)

4. Read the caption for the photograph on page 10. Why do farmers in Iowa grow a great deal of corn? (Iowa has the right climate and land for corn.)

5. Read page 11. What three things play an important role in productivity? (capital, education, and technology)

Advanced Level Questions

Encourage students at this level to provide written responses in complete sentences to the following questions.

1. What is the difference between wants and needs? (Needs are things people must have to survive. Wants are things that people desire.)

2. How are goods and services different? (Goods are things you can see, touch, and buy or sell. A service is any work that someone does for others for money.)

3. Why are natural resources important for production? (Natural resources are used to produce all kinds of goods and services.)

4. Why do most workers specialize? (When people specialize, they are able to produce more.)

5. Why are well-educated workers more productive? (Well-educated employees are better able to solve problems, understand electronics, and operate complicated machinery.)

Closing the Chapter

Distribute copies of the Outline found on page 55 of this guide. Ask students to use the headings and information from the chapter to complete the outline. Then, have students use the outline to write a summary of what they have learned in the chapter.

Topic: What Is Economics?
I. Wants, Needs, Goods, and Services
   A. _____
   B. _____
II. The Four Factors of Production
   A. _____
   B. _____
   C. _____
   D. _____
III. Opportunity Costs
   A. _____
   B. _____
IV. Specialization
   A. _____
   B. _____
V. Productivity
   A. _____
   B. _____
   C. _____
   D. _____

Chapter 2 · Economic Systems

pages 16–29

▶ Introducing the Chapter

Tapping Prior Knowledge
Ask students to look at the photograph on page 16 of the Student Edition and describe what they see. Then, have students compare and contrast this market with places where their families buy food, clothing, and other necessities. Ask students, *How are they alike? How are they different?* Explain that Chapter 2 describes different types of economic systems and how they provide people with the things they need to live.

Preteaching Vocabulary
Personalizing Vocabulary Have students form small groups. Have each group look for ten unfamiliar words or phrases from different sections of the chapter. Once groups have identified these words or phrases, ask them to record the words or phrases in their Word Logs and to use their bilingual dictionaries to define them.

Identifying Essential Vocabulary Go over the pronunciation and meaning of each word or phrase in the box below. Then, ask each student to write a sentence for each word or phrase. Ask students to rewrite their sentences, leaving a blank space in place of the vocabulary term. Have students trade sentences with a partner and fill in the blanks in the sentences their partner wrote.

Word or Phrase	Meaning
stalls	small booths (p. 18)
boomerangs	flat, curved sticks that can be thrown so that they return to the thrower (p. 18)
follow in their fathers' footsteps	work in the same jobs as their fathers (p. 19)
not a pure market economy	not completely a market system (p. 21)
regulate	to control according to a rule (p. 21)
unrest and upheaval	trouble and disturbances (p. 24)
revolt	a rebelling against the government or any authority (p. 27)

▶ Applying Content Knowledge

From the Chapter: The Changing Economic World: Economic Systems (page 24)
Ask students to read The Changing Economic World: Economic Systems on page 24 of the Student Edition. Have students pick one of the nations listed in the feature and conduct further research on that nation's current economic system. Students may conduct research in the library or on the Internet.

Organizing Information
Distribute copies of the Venn Diagram found on page 57 of this guide. Have students entitle their diagram **Economic Systems**. Then, as students read the chapter, ask them to use the diagram to compare and contrast a market economy and a mixed economy. Remind students to use details from the chapter to show the main traits of each system.

Role-Playing
Call on a volunteer to play the part of a person living in a traditional economic system, such as the ones described on pages 18 and 19 of the Student Edition. Ask this student to describe his or her traditional lifestyle and how people meet their economic needs and wants under this system. Next, have another volunteer act as if he or she lives in a pure command economy, such as the one described on pages 22 and 23 of the Student Edition. Ask this volunteer to tell how the government affects how people work and what they can buy and sell. Finally, have a volunteer describe everyday life in the U.S. market economy.

Personalizing the Lesson
Have students reread the six major characteristics of a market economy that are listed on pages 21 and 22 of the Student Edition. Ask them to write each characteristic at the top of a sheet of paper. Then, have students write examples of each characteristic, based on their own experience or that of a member of their family or community. A student example of the fourth characteristic—*people have economic freedom of choice*—might be someone who has changed jobs recently.

Assessing Content Knowledge

Ask students to respond to the following questions. You may wish to encourage students with higher language proficiency to help beginning level students understand the questions.

Beginning Level Questions

Encourage students at this level to think about the answers to these questions and to offer short verbal responses.

1. Look at page 18. What kind of government system helps to satisfy its peoples' needs and wants? (an economic system)

2. Read the bottom of page 19. True or false: Another name for a market economic system is capitalism. (true)

3. Look at page 21. In a market economy, do individuals or the government own most businesses? (individuals)

4. Turn to page 23. Does the government or the people control the economy in a command system? (the government)

5. Look at page 26. Is the standard of living high or low in a healthy economy? (high)

Intermediate Level Questions

Encourage students at this level to offer verbal responses or short written responses to the following questions.

1. Read the Words to Know on page 17. What is profit? (the money made by a business or person after all costs have been paid)

2. Read page 18. What are the three basic types of economic systems? (traditional, market, and command systems)

3. Read page 22. Which market economy characteristic relates to making a profit? (Businesses are allowed to succeed.)

4. Read page 23. What kind of economic system did Russia have for more than 70 years? (a command economic system)

5. Read page 26. What is one way to measure whether good food, shelter, education, and healthcare are available to the people in a country? (the standard of living)

Advanced Level Questions

Encourage students at this level to provide written responses in complete sentences to the following questions.

1. What goods and services does a traditional economic system usually produce? (A traditional economic system produces the goods and services that were produced in the past.)

2. What is the main difference between a market economic system and a command system? (In a market system, individuals control the production of goods; in a command system, the government does.)

3. Explain why the market system in the United States is not considered "pure." (The U.S. government has some say in how goods and services are made and sold in order to protect the health and safety of its people.)

4. What does it mean to have economic freedom of choice? (People are free to choose their own jobs and to buy and sell the goods the way they want.)

5. What kind of economy would you expect in a country with a high standard of living? (The economy would be a strong one, able to provide the jobs, goods, and services that are needed.)

▶ Closing the Chapter

Distribute copies of the Four-Column Chart found on page 52 of this guide. Have students entitle the chart **Economic Systems** and label the columns **Traditional**, **Market**, **Command**, and **Mixed**. Then, have students work with a partner to fill in their charts with key ideas and details from Chapter 2 that describe each type of economic system. Ask students to use their completed charts to write a summary about what they have learned.

Topic: Economic Systems

Traditional	Market	Command	Mixed

Chapter 3 — Consumers and Demand

▶ Introducing the Chapter

Tapping Prior Knowledge

Show students some sales flyers for a local retail store. Ask volunteers to read the advertisements aloud. Then, have them explain in their own words why stores sometimes put goods on sale. Finally, have students write the four main headings of the chapter as questions: *What is the law of demand? What can change demand? How do income and substitute goods affect demand? How do complementary goods affect demand?* Students should take notes while reading the sections to answer these four questions.

Preteaching Vocabulary

Personalizing Vocabulary Begin by asking students to preview the chapter for five unfamiliar words or phrases and to record them in their Word Logs. Ask students to use their bilingual dictionaries to define the words or phrases.

Identifying Essential Vocabulary Go over the pronunciation and meaning of each word or phrase in the box below. Next, ask students to work with a partner to write the sentence where they find the word or phrase in the chapter and then to replace the word or phrase with a familiar word or phrase.

Word or Phrase	Meaning
prices slashed	prices lowered a great deal (p. 33)
bargain	something sold at a favorable price for the buyer (p. 33)
storewide	in the whole store (p. 33)
to cover the action	to report on events (p. 34)
in high demand	wanted by many people (p. 35)
sunbonnets	hats women wore to shade themselves from bright sunlight (p. 36)
got raises	had their pay increased (p. 39)
economically independent	able to meet one's own wants and needs (p. 42)
rapidly industrializing	building many new factories (p. 42)

▶ Applying Content Knowledge

From the Chapter: Great Economic Thinkers: Quett Masire (page 42)

Ask students to read Great Economic Thinkers: Quett Masire on page 42 of the Student Edition. Tell students that some people in Botswana considered Masire a great leader. Ask students to share information about a great leader from another country. *Why are they great leaders? What makes a great leader different from other kinds of leaders?* Next, distribute copies of the Venn Diagram found on page 57 of this guide. Ask students to label the left circle **Quett Masire**, the right circle **My Great Leader** (the name of the great leader from the country of their choice), and the middle section **Both.** Then, have students compare and contrast Quett Masire with the great leader that they chose. Have students use their completed Venn diagrams to write a summary. Students may wish to begin their paragraphs with the following sentence: **Quett Masire and _____ are similar to each other because. . . .**

Using Visuals

Ask students to look at the illustration of the woman on page 37 of the Student Edition and discuss the clothing styles of the early 1900s. Then, have students create their own illustrations of a type of clothing or object that was once popular or fashionable but is no longer so. For example, students might draw a special toy that everyone wanted one holiday season. Ask students to describe how demand for the items that they have drawn have changed over time.

Using Realia

Ask students to look again at examples of sales flyers or advertisements that announce large sales. Have students discuss among themselves how these ads are likely to affect demand. Then, have students create a hypothetical demand curve graph for one of the advertised products. Students should write a short paragraph under their graph to explain the reason for the curve.

Assessing Content Knowledge

Ask students to respond to the following questions. You may wish to encourage students with higher language proficiency to help beginning level students understand the questions.

Beginning Level Questions

Encourage students at this level to think about the answers to these questions and to offer short verbal responses.

1. Look at the Words to Know on page 33. What is the amount of money that a person makes in a certain period of time called? (income)

2. Read page 34. Are consumers able to buy more or less when prices go down? (more)

3. Look at page 35. What does the graph show a demand for? (Cal's Custom T's)

4. Read page 36. Can demand for a product like T-shirts change over time? (yes)

5. Read pages 39 and 40. Are substitute goods interchangeable or complementary? (interchangeable)

Intermediate Level Questions

Encourage students at this level to offer verbal responses or short written responses to the following questions.

1. Look at the Words to Know on page 33. What is demand? (the amount of a good or service that consumers are willing and able to buy at a certain price)

2. Read page 34. What does the law of demand state? (Consumers are usually willing and able to buy more if prices go down.)

3. Look at Graph 3.1 on page 35. How many T-shirts could Cal sell if he charged $30 each? (20 T-shirts)

4. Look at page 38. Which graph shows an increase in demand for Cal's T-shirts? (Graph 3.2)

5. Read page 39. How does an increase in income usually affect demand for goods? (An increase in income usually increases demand.)

Advanced Level Questions

Encourage students at this level to provide written responses in complete sentences to the following questions.

1. Look at the photograph on page 32. Why might these girls' demand for clothing be higher than usual? (The clothing is on sale so they might buy more.)

2. Look at Graph 3.1 on page 35. How does price affect demand for Cal's T's? (As the price of the T-shirts decreases, the demand increases.)

3. According to Graph 3.2 on page 38, how many T-shirts does Cal sell at $30 once demand shifts to the right? (35)

4. Suppose the price of butter increases. Why would the demand for margarine also probably increase? (Margarine is a substitute for butter, so people would demand more of it to avoid buying butter.)

5. Why do consumers not affect demand in a command economy? (In a command economy, the government decides how many goods to make and what the price will be.)

▶ Closing the Chapter

Ask students to look at the notes they took for the Tapping Prior Knowledge activity on page 6 of this guide. Have students use these notes to create a two-column chart. Distribute copies of the Two-Column Chart found on page 50 of this guide. Students should write **Consumers and Demand** as the topic, label the columns **Question** and **Answer**, and write the four questions as shown below, in the left column of the chart. Then, direct them to write their answers to these questions in the right column. Finally, have students use their answers to write a summary of the main ideas of Chapter 3.

Topic: Consumers and Demand

Question	Answer
What is the law of demand?	
What can change demand?	
How do income and substitute goods affect demand?	
How do complementary goods affect demand?	

Chapter 4 — Producers and Supply

pages 46–55

▶ Introducing the Chapter

Tapping Prior Knowledge

Ask students if they have ever bought some item that later became very popular. Ask them how they think the producer of that item reacted when he or she realized the great demand for it. Next, explain the law of supply to students. Then, have students look at Graph 4.1 on page 49 of the Student Edition. Finally, ask students, *What might cause Cal to supply more of his hand-painted T-shirts to his customers?*

Preteaching Vocabulary

Personalizing Vocabulary Begin by asking students to preview the chapter for five unfamiliar words or phrases and to record them in their Word Logs. Ask students to use their bilingual dictionaries to define the words or phrases.

Identifying Essential Vocabulary Go over the pronunciation and meaning of each word or phrase in the box below. Then, ask students to work with a partner to write the sentence where they find the word or phrase in the chapter and then to replace the word or phrase with a familiar word or phrase. Students may wish to consult their bilingual dictionaries as they rewrite the sentences.

Word or Phrase	Meaning
holding a meeting	having a meeting (p. 47)
look over	review (p. 47)
furthermore	in addition (p. 47)
take a loss	lose money (p. 48)
cover the cost	provide the money for (p. 49)
more brilliant	brighter (p. 51)
custom hats	handmade hats (p. 52)
phase out	stop gradually (p. 52)
figure into	have an effect on (p. 52)
outweigh	to be more important than (p. 52)

▶ Applying Content Knowledge

From the Chapter: Economic Decision Making: Labor Supply (page 52)

Ask students to read Economic Decision Making: Labor Supply on page 52 of the Student Edition. Then, ask students to suppose they have started a small business, such as making homemade pies. Ask them to role-play a business meeting in which they decide how many pies they would need to produce to make a profit. In their discussions, students should mention the costs of production and how new technology might change their business.

Using Visuals

Ask students to look at the graphs on pages 49, 50, and 51 of the Student Edition. Have students make copies on graph paper of the supply curves shown in Graphs 4.1, 4.2., and 4.3. Then, have students work in groups to determine what we can learn about the law of supply from these graphs. Ask students, *What does the supply curve mean in general? Why does the curve shift to the left or to the right?*

Organizing Information

Distribute copies of the Spider Web found on page 54 of this guide. Students should use as a topic for the web **Producers and Supply**, and they should label the corners of the web **The Law of Supply**, **Costs of Production**, **New Technology**, and **Opportunity Costs**. Have students note important ideas and details as they read each section of the chapter.

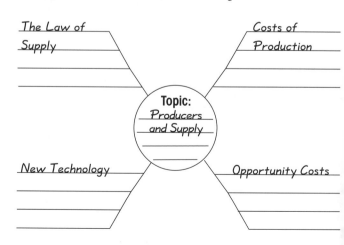

Assessing Content Knowledge

Ask students to respond to the following questions. You may wish to encourage students with higher language proficiency to help beginning level students understand the questions.

Beginning Level Questions

Encourage students at this level to think about the answers to these questions and to offer short verbal responses.

1. Look at the Words to Know on page 47. Does an executive or a salesperson direct and manage a business? (an executive)

2. Read page 48. Are higher prices an incentive for producers to produce more or less? (more)

3. Look at Graph 4.1 on page 49. What kind of curve does it show? (a supply curve)

4. Read pages 49 and 50. Does supply go up or down when costs of production go up? (down)

5. Read page 51. Does new technology usually increase or decrease supply? (increase)

Intermediate Level Questions

Encourage students at this level to offer verbal responses or short written responses to the following questions.

1. Read the Words to Know on page 47. What is an incentive? (something that encourages people to work harder or to produce more)

2. Read page 48. What does the law of supply state? (When the price of a good or service rises, producers will usually be willing to supply more of that good or service.)

3. Look at Graph 4.1 on page 49. How many $10 T-shirts would Cal supply per semester? (10 T-shirts)

4. Read page 50 and look at Graph 4.2. Why has the supply curve shifted to the left? (Cal's costs of production have increased.)

5. Look at Graph 4.3 on page 51. How does new technology affect the supply of T-shirts? (It increases the supply.)

Advanced Level Questions

Encourage students at this level to provide written responses in complete sentences to the following questions.

1. When are producers willing to increase the supply of the goods and services they sell? (Producers increase the supply of goods and services when prices for the goods and services rise.)

2. Suppose the cost of plain white T-shirts fell. How might Cal change the supply of his custom T-shirts? (He would probably increase the supply of his custom T-shirts.)

3. Which supply curve—Graph 4.2 on page 50 or Graph 4.3 on page 51—shows an increase in supply? (Graph 4.3 shows an increase in supply.)

4. Why might Cal give up making T-shirts and start making hats? (He can make a greater profit from hats.)

5. What three things can affect the supply of goods and services? (The costs of production, technology, and opportunity costs affect supply.)

Closing the Chapter

Distribute copies of the Two-Column Chart found on page 50 of this guide. Have students entitle the chart **Producers and Supply**, label the columns **Cause** and **Effect** and write the four sentences as shown below, in the left column of the chart. Ask students to complete the chart using information from Chapter 4. Then, ask them to write a summary of the causes and effects that they have charted.

Topic: Producers and Supply

Cause	Effect
The price of a good rises.	
The costs of production rise, but prices stay the same.	
New technology makes it cheaper to produce goods.	

Chapter 5 — How Prices Are Determined

▶ Introducing the Chapter

Tapping Prior Knowledge

Have students look at the photograph on page 56 of the Student Edition. Ask students if they have ever gone to a flea market or garage sale and bargained about the price of something they wanted to buy. Have students describe the process of how the price was determined. Then, ask students to preview Chapter 5, reading the Words to Know on page 57 and the headings throughout the chapter. Point out the graphs on pages 59, 60, and 61. Ask students how these graphs are different from the graphs they studied in Chapters 3 and 4. Elicit that these graphs show curves for both the supply and the demand for Cal's T-shirts.

Preteaching Vocabulary

Personalizing Vocabulary Begin by asking students to preview the chapter for five unfamiliar words or phrases and to record them in their Word Logs. Ask students to use their bilingual dictionaries to define the words or phrases.

Identifying Essential Vocabulary Go over the pronunciation and meaning of each word or phrase in the box below. Then, ask students to work with a partner to write the sentence where they find the word or phrase in the chapter and then to replace the word or phrase with a familiar word or phrase.

Word or Phrase	Meaning
flea market	a type of market that usually sells cheap goods (p. 57)
make up his mind	decide (p. 57)
consumer	buyer (p. 58)
it is rare	it does not happen very often (p. 58)
reduce	lower (p. 61)
to keep up with demand	to meet the demand (p. 63)
odd jobs	part-time jobs (p. 64)
be better off	be in a better condition (p. 64)

▶ Applying Content Knowledge

From the Chapter: Learning Objectives (page 56)

Call on students to read aloud the four Learning Objectives on page 56 of the Student Edition. Invite volunteers to write the four objectives on the board. Then, as students finish reading each section of the text, call on students to say a few sentences that show they have met each objective.

Using Manipulatives

Divide the class into small groups. Have students work together to make a graph like Graph 5.1 on page 59 of the Student Edition. Students should reproduce the labels and numbers that appear along the *x*-axis and *y*-axis of the graph. Then, ask students to cut small strips of yellow and blue paper to represent the supply curve and the demand curve. Next, have students place these curves in different locations on the graph. After each location, students should sketch the graph on a sheet of paper and interpret what it means in a short paragraph. Students should demonstrate an understanding of how small or large surpluses or shortages might develop depending on the placement of the supply and demand curves.

Personalizing the Lesson

Have students write a few sentences that tell about a shopping experience in which they took advantage of a great sale. Have students tell the original price of the product and how much it was reduced. Ask students to use the terms *surplus, inventory,* and *equilibrium price* to describe the experience. Call on volunteers to read their narratives aloud.

Summarizing

Ask students to work in groups to list the main ideas of the chapter. Have students use their lists to write a summary of the chapter. Ask for volunteers to read their summaries aloud.

Assessing Content Knowledge

Ask students to respond to the following questions. You may wish to encourage students with higher language proficiency to help beginning level students understand the questions.

Beginning Level Questions

Encourage students at this level to think about the answers to these questions and to offer short verbal responses.

1. Look at the photograph on page 56. Where are these people? (at a flea market)

2. Look at the Words to Know on page 57. What are products that a business has in stock called? (inventory)

3. Look at the Words to Know on page 57. True or false: When two things cross at a point, they intersect. (true)

4. Look at Graph 5.1 on page 59. Which curve shows supply—the green curve or the blue curve? (the green curve)

5. Look at the photograph and caption on page 62. What is this store doing to reduce its inventory? (having a sale)

Intermediate Level Questions

Encourage students at this level to offer verbal responses or short written responses to the following questions.

1. Read page 59. What is an equilibrium price? (the price at which the amount demanded equals the amount supplied)

2. Look at Graph 5.1 on page 59. What equilibrium price is shown for a T-shirt? ($20)

3. Read page 61. Is a surplus too many or too few goods? (too many goods)

4. Read pages 62 and 63. What develops when the prices of goods are below the equilibrium price? (a shortage)

5. Look at Graph 5.4 on page 63. How much should Cal charge for a T-shirt to avoid a shortage? ($20)

Advanced Level Questions

Encourage students at this level to provide written responses in complete sentences to the following questions.

1. What determines the prices of the goods we buy? (The forces of supply and demand work together to determine prices.)

2. How do producers feel about the equilibrium price for their goods? (They are satisfied with their profits at the equilibrium price.)

3. What causes a surplus of goods to develop? (A surplus develops when the price of goods is higher than the amount consumers are willing to pay for the goods.)

4. What usually happens to end a surplus of goods? (Sellers lower their prices so consumers will buy the surplus goods.)

5. What causes a shortage of goods? (A shortage develops when buyers want to buy more goods than sellers are willing to sell at a certain price.)

Closing the Chapter

Distribute copies of the Main Idea and Supporting Details Chart found on page 58 of this guide. Have students provide the following statement as the main idea: **The forces of supply and demand work together to determine price every day.** Then, ask students to label the supporting detail boxes **Equilibrium Price, Surplus, Inventory,** and **Shortage.** Students should fill these boxes with notes about each of these terms. Finally, in the summary box, have students write a short paragraph to summarize the main ideas of Chapter 5.

MAIN IDEA

The forces of supply and demand work together to determine price every day.

SUPPORTING DETAILS

Equilibrium Price	Surplus	Inventory	Shortage

SUMMARY

Chapter 6 ▷ American Business pages 70–83

▷ Introducing the Chapter

Tapping Prior Knowledge
Ask students to preview the chapter by reading the headings and the Words to Know and their definitions on page 71 of the Student Edition. Have students look at the photographs on pages 70 and 76 of the Student Edition and discuss what type of business each of these people own. Then, have students look at the photograph and caption of the oil tanker on page 78 of the Student Edition. Discuss how a large oil company might be different from the businesses pictured in the earlier photographs.

Preteaching Vocabulary
Personalizing Vocabulary Have students form small groups. Have each group look for ten unfamiliar words or phrases from different sections of the chapter. Once groups have identified these words or phrases, ask them to record the words or phrases in their Word Logs and to use their bilingual dictionaries to define them.

Identifying Essential Vocabulary Go over the pronunciation and meaning of each word or phrase in the box below. Next, distribute an index card to each student. Ask students to write a question on the index card using one or more of the vocabulary terms. Then, have students exchange cards with a partner and answer their partner's question.

Word or Phrase	Meaning
catch her ride	meet someone who will drive her (p. 71)
waits on tables	works as a waiter in a restaurant (p. 71)
dock your pay	withhold money from your pay (p. 71)
be their own boss	work for themselves (p. 74)
takes the plunge	decides to move forward (p. 75)
entitle	allow (p. 77)
looks very bright	looks successful (p. 77)

▷ Applying Content Knowledge

From the Chapter: Remember (page 72)
Ask students to read the Remember feature in the margin of page 72 of the Student Edition. Point out that it reminds them of the meaning of *income*. Then, ask students to survey Chapter 6 for other terms that they have learned in previous chapters, such as *profit, entrepreneurs, free market economic system,* and *incentive.* Have students write Remember facts for these terms on index cards or on self-adhesive notes that can be placed near where the terms appear in the textbook.

Organizing Information
Ask students to use the chapter headings to create a list of questions about the chapter. For example, the heading The Circular Flow of Income could become the question **What is the circular flow of income?** Then, ask students to answer each of these questions.

Personalizing the Lesson
Tell students that a five-dollar bill that they spent at a local store last month was returned to them 3 months later in the pay they received for a part-time job. Then, have them create a poster that documents this circular flow of income, including all possible places the money may have been while it was out of the students' possession.

Summarizing
Ask students to work in pairs to read and answer the Check Your Understanding questions on pages 73, 74, and 79 of the Student Edition. Suggest that students alternate reading and answering the questions. Have students use their answers to write two or more paragraphs that summarize the chapter. Students may use their summaries to review Chapter 6 of the Student Edition.

Assessing Content Knowledge

Ask students to respond to the following questions. You may wish to encourage students with higher language proficiency to help beginning level students understand the questions.

Beginning Level Questions

Encourage students at this level to think about the answers to these questions and to offer short verbal responses.

1. Look at the Words to Know on page 71. Is stock a share of ownership in a corporation? (yes)

2. Look at the diagram on page 73. What does the diagram show? (the circular flow of income)

3. Read page 74. Is money that a business brings in called revenue or loss? (revenue)

4. Read page 75. Is a partnership one of the three main types of businesses? (yes)

5. Read page 77. Who owns the shares of stock of a corporation? (stockholders or shareholders)

Intermediate Level Questions

Encourage students at this level to offer verbal responses or short written responses to the following questions.

1. Look at the diagram on page 73. Where do wages paid by businesses flow to? (to households)

2. Read page 74. True or false: Many people start small businesses because they want to "be their own boss." (true)

3. Read page 75. What are the three main types of businesses? (sole proprietorship, partnership, and corporation)

4. Look at the table on page 79. What are two disadvantages to being the sole proprietor of a business? (Possible answers: Sometimes it is hard to raise money; the owner is responsible for the success or failure of the business; the owner takes personal risk of being sued.)

5. Look again at the table on page 79. What are two advantages of a partnership? (Partners share work; partners can contribute money to help the business succeed.)

Advanced Level Questions

Encourage students at this level to provide written responses in complete sentences to the following questions.

1. What is the circular flow of money? (Consumers pay money to businesses to buy goods and services. Businesses pay money to workers for their labor.)

2. How is a sole proprietorship different from a partnership? (One person owns a sole proprietorship, whereas a partnership is owned by two or more people.)

3. What is a corporation? (A corporation is a business that has been divided into shares of stock.)

4. How do corporations raise money? (Corporations raise money through the sale of stock.)

5. Why do corporations give dividends to shareholders? (Dividends are a way to share the corporation's profits among shareholders.)

Closing the Chapter

Distribute copies of the Three-Column Chart found on page 51 of this guide. Ask students to create a chart entitled **Types of Businesses** with the headings **Sole Proprietorship**, **Partnership**, and **Corporation**. Tell students to complete their charts by reading pages 75–78 of the Student Edition. Students should note important details about each type of business in the appropriate column. Then, ask students to write a summary about different types of businesses.

Topic: Types of Businesses

Sole Proprietorship	Partnership	Corporation

Chapter 7

Stocks and Bonds

pages 84–97

▶ Introducing the Chapter

Tapping Prior Knowledge
Encourage students to share what they know about the stock market. Ask students, *Have you heard stock market updates on TV or radio news? Why do you think people might be interested in hearing about whether the stock market is up or down throughout each day?*

Preteaching Vocabulary
Personalizing Vocabulary Have students form small groups. Have each group look for ten unfamiliar words or phrases from different sections of the chapter. Once groups have identified these words or phrases, ask them to record the words or phrases in their Word Logs and to use their bilingual dictionaries to define them. As a class, the groups may share their Word Logs.

Identifying Essential Vocabulary Go over the pronunciation and meaning of each phrase in the box below. Then, ask students to work with a partner to write the sentence where they find the phrase in the chapter and then to replace the phrase with a familiar word or phrase. Students may wish to consult their bilingual dictionaries as they rewrite the sentences.

Word or Phrase	Meaning
a high return	a high interest rate (p. 86)
short of money	not having enough money (p. 86)
drive the price up	make the price go up (p. 87)
buy or sell orders	orders to buy or sell stock (p. 88)
flying upward/ tumbling downward	moving up quickly/falling quickly (p. 89)
skyrocket in value	become much more valuable (p. 92)
inside information	information that is not available to the public (p. 92)
fortune-tellers	people who think they can predict the future (p. 92)

▶ Applying Content Knowledge

From the Chapter: Learn More About It: Reading the Stock Report (pages 94 and 95)
Ask students to read the feature Learn More About It: Reading the Stock Report on pages 94 and 95 of the Student Edition. Then, provide recent copies of a daily newspaper published in your region. Have students find the business section of the paper. Ask them to look for news about the stock market and read its headlines. Students should look for a particular stock or bond and interpret its information in a short paragraph.

Summarizing
Ask students to work in pairs to read and answer the Check Your Understanding questions on pages 87 and 89 of the Student Edition. Suggest that students alternate reading and answering the questions. Have students use their answers to write two or more paragraphs that summarize the chapter. Students may use their summaries to review Chapter 7 of the Student Edition.

Personalizing the Lesson
Discuss with students products that they like or use. Ask them to name the companies that make and sell these goods. Alternately, students may name some large companies that employ many people locally. Help students to find these companies in the stock report of the newspaper. Tell students that they own 100 shares of stock of the company of their choice. Then, have students keep track of the price of the stock over the course of a week. At week's end, have the students figure out how much money they would have made or lost. Ask them to write a summary of their experience in a short paragraph.

Assessing Content Knowledge

Ask students to respond to the following questions. You may wish to encourage students with higher language proficiency to help beginning level students understand the questions.

Beginning Level Questions

Encourage students at this level to think about the answers to these questions and to offer short verbal responses.

1. Look at the photograph on page 84. What are the people shown in the picture doing? (buying and selling stocks at the New York Stock Exchange)

2. Read page 87. Does a good investment give you a capital loss or gain? (gain)

3. Read page 88. Where are most stocks traded? (in a stock market)

4. Read page 90. Do corporations and governments borrow money using bonds or stocks? (bonds)

5. Read page 92. Can buying stocks and bonds be risky? (yes)

Intermediate Level Questions

Encourage students at this level to offer verbal responses or short written responses to the following questions.

1. Look at the photograph and caption on page 84. Why is this place important to the U.S. economy? (Possible answer: It is the main place where people ask brokers to invest their money.)

2. Read page 86. If you wanted to be sure of getting dividends, would you buy common stock or preferred stock? (preferred stock)

3. Read page 92. What part of government regulates stocks and bonds? (the Securities and Exchange Commission, or SEC)

4. Look at the stock report on page 94. What does the heading "Net chg" mean? (It means "net change," which tells you whether the stock increased or decreased in price from the day before.)

5. Look again at the stock report on page 94. What dividend did Vivir preferred stock pay? ($2.12)

Advanced Level Questions

Encourage students at this level to provide written responses in complete sentences to the following questions.

1. How is preferred stock different from common stock? (Preferred stock offers stated dividends; common stock may not pay dividends. Owners of common stock have voting rights, whereas owners of preferred stock do not.)

2. When would a person have a capital loss after selling stock? (A person who sold stock for less than it cost when it was bought would have a capital loss.)

3. If the stock market is "up," how do people feel about the U.S. economy? (It is a sign that people feel confident about business and that the economy is strong.)

4. In what ways are bonds safer than stocks? (The prices of bonds don't go up and down as much as stocks; a bond buyer is guaranteed the face value of the bond at maturity.)

5. Why is it important to have a stockbroker you can trust? (The broker will be handling your money and giving you advice about what stocks to buy and sell.)

▶ Closing the Chapter

Distribute copies of the Venn Diagram found on page 57 of this guide. Ask students to fill in the Venn diagram. Use the chapter title, **Stocks and Bonds**, as the topic. Place the heading **Stocks** in the left circle. Place the heading **Bonds** in the right circle. Where the circles overlap, students should label the section **Both**. Next, ask students to list key details that they learned about each heading. Students may wish to use some of the Words to Know listed on page 85 of the Student Edition when appropriate. Then, have students use the completed Venn diagram to write a summary about what they learned in the chapter.

Topic: Stocks and Bonds

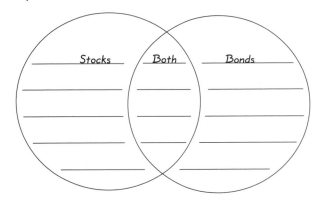

Chapter 8 Competition

pages 98–111

▶ Introducing the Chapter

Tapping Prior Knowledge

Ask students to preview the chapter by reading the headings and by looking at the photographs and chart. Draw students' attention to the title of the chapter, "Competition." Ask students, *What do you associate with the word* competition? Students might mention that sports teams and athletes are in competitions. Then, ask students, *How might producers of goods and stores compete for customers?* Finally, have students read the definition for *competition* and *perfect competition* in the Words to Know on page 99 of the Student Edition.

Preteaching Vocabulary

Personalizing Vocabulary Begin by asking students to preview the chapter for five unfamiliar words or phrases and to record them in their Word Logs. Ask students to use their bilingual dictionaries to define the words or phrases.

Identifying Essential Vocabulary Go over the pronunciation and meaning of each word or phrase in the box below. Then, ask students to work with a partner to write the sentence where they find the word or phrase in the chapter and then to replace the word or phrase with a familiar word or phrase.

Word or Phrase	Meaning
we're all set	we are ready (p. 99)
sheepishly	in an embarrassed way (p. 99)
offered good service	treated customers well (p. 100)
the better deal	the cheaper price (p. 100)
the going price	the usual price (p. 101)
next to impossible	almost impossible (p. 104)
see what you run into	see what happens (p. 104)
a competitive edge	a feature that sets a product apart from the competition (p. 106)

▶ Applying Content Knowledge

From the Chapter: Degrees of Competition (page 107)

Ask students to look at the chart Degrees of Competition on page 107 of the Student Edition. Ask students, *How easy is it to start a business in which there is perfect competition? What is the effect on prices when there are many producers of a good?* Write students' answers on the board or ask students to record the answers on their own sheets of paper.

Using Visuals

Have students look at the opening photograph on page 98 of the Student Edition, and have them describe what they see. Ask students, *How might a customer pick a seller at this produce market?* Encourage students to discuss how they select which gas stations, grocery stores, or fast-food restaurants at which to shop in their communities. Elicit from students the ways in which like businesses differentiate themselves from one another.

Organizing Information

Distribute copies of the Three-Column Chart found on page 51 of this guide. Ask students to label the topic **Types of Competition** and the headings **Perfect Competition**, **Limited Competition**, and **Monopoly**. As students read pages 101–106 of the Student Edition, ask them to take notes about each type of competition in the appropriate column. When students have finished their charts, they may compare them with the information listed in the chart on page 107 of the Student Edition.

Using Realia

Have students find advertisements in newspapers or magazines that show products or services made by a small number of sellers, such as cars or appliances. Ask students to distinguish how the seller uses advertising to get a competitive edge over its competition. Ask students, *Is this advertisement persuasive? Is this product really different from its competition? What would make you buy or not buy this product?*

Assessing Content Knowledge

Ask students to respond to the following questions. You may wish to encourage students with higher language proficiency to help beginning level students understand the questions.

Beginning Level Questions

Encourage students at this level to think about the answers to these questions and to offer short verbal responses.

1. Read Economic Competition on page 100. Does competition occur between businesses that have similar goods and services or similar profits? (similar goods and services)

2. Read Perfect Competition on pages 101 and 102. Is producers selling the same good or service a characteristic of perfect competition? (yes)

3. Look at the photograph and caption on page 101. What kind of competition does this product have? (perfect competition)

4. Read Monopoly on pages 102 and 103. In a monopoly, how many producers are there? (one)

5. Look at the photograph and caption on page 105. What kind of competition does this appliance company have? (limited)

Intermediate Level Questions

Encourage students at this level to offer verbal responses or short written responses to the following questions.

1. Read page 100. What is one reason why competition is a key force in the U.S. economy? (Possible answers: Competition forces businesses to supply goods and services that people want; competition forces businesses to sell those goods and services at prices close to the cost of making them.)

2. Read pages 101 and 102. Is it easy or difficult to find information about prices, quality, and the availability of goods or services when you have perfect competition? (easy)

3. Read page 102. What do you have when there is no competition? (a monopoly)

4. Read page 103. What 1890 U.S. law outlawed most monopolies? (the Sherman Anti-Trust Act)

5. Read page 105. What type of competition is found among makers of cars? (limited competition)

Advanced Level Questions

Encourage students at this level to provide written responses in complete sentences to the following questions.

1. What tends to be true of any goods offered for sale under perfect competition? (They vary only slightly; they are basically identical.)

2. Why can't the owner of a monopoly charge any price he or she wants to? (There may not be a demand for a product or service at too high a price.)

3. Why is competition limited among makers of cars, washing machines, or refrigerators? (A small number of sellers make these goods; it is hard to start up a business to make these products.)

4. What is true of products made by only a few producers, such as cars? (The products and their prices tend to be very similar.)

5. What are some ways in which companies can distinguish themselves from the competition? (Possible answers: better service, warranties, more options or styles, better advertising)

Closing the Chapter

Distribute copies of the Outline found on page 55 of this guide. Have students review the chapter to fill in the headings and corresponding details. Once the outline is completed, ask students to use it to summarize what they learned in the chapter.

Topic: Competition
I. The Benefits of Economic Competition
  A. _____
  B. _____
II. Characteristics of Perfect Competition
  A. _____
  B. _____
  C. _____
  D. _____
III. Characteristics of Monopolies
  A. _____
  B. _____
  C. _____
IV. Benefits of Limited Competition
  A. _____
  B. _____

Chapter 9

Workers and Wages
pages 112–123

▶ Introducing the Chapter

Tapping Prior Knowledge

Ask students to share their experiences in the workforce, such as babysitting jobs or working behind a cash register, they may have had and how much they earned in wages at these jobs. Show students the classified section of a local newspaper and have volunteers read selected "Help Wanted" advertisements. Ask them what the wages for the jobs are, if specified. Based on the chapter title, have students make predictions about what they will learn in the chapter.

Preteaching Vocabulary

Personalizing Vocabulary Have students form small groups. Have each group look for ten unfamiliar words or phrases from different sections of the chapter. Once groups have identified these words or phrases, ask them to record the words or phrases in their Word Logs and to use their bilingual dictionaries to define them.

Identifying Essential Vocabulary Go over the pronunciation and meaning of each phrase in the box below. Then, ask each student to write a sentence for each word or phrase. Ask students to rewrite their sentences, leaving a blank space in place of the vocabulary term. Have students trade sentences with a partner and fill in the blanks in the sentences written by the partner.

Word or Phrase	Meaning
take certain steps	do specific things (p. 114)
pretty much count on	expect (p. 115)
jobs were secure	jobs that did not end (p. 115)
to pursue such a career	to prepare for a specific career (p. 117)
bachelor's degree	four-year college degree (p. 117)
on one level/on a broader level	from one viewpoint/from a wider viewpoint (p. 118)
to ensure	to make sure of (p. 119)

▶ Applying Content Knowledge

From the Chapter: Photographs (pages 112, 116, and 119)

Ask students to look at the photographs of the steelworkers on page 112, the medical technician on page 116, and the auto factory robots on page 119 of the Student Edition. Ask students to discuss the skills and training needed and the potential wages for each job. Then, have students search through magazines for photographs of different workers at their jobs. Have students create a poster with illustrations of the jobs they find. Each illustration should be labeled with the name of the job, a job description, level of training and education needed, and the potential wages to be earned at the job. Students should try to find a wide range of jobs that require varying degrees of skills and education. Ask volunteers to present their posters to the class. You also may want to display posters in the classroom.

Using Realia

Ask pairs of students to check the Help Wanted advertisements in the classified section of a local newspaper or an online listing of jobs. Have students note what types of jobs seem most available in their community or region. Then, ask students to name three occupations or careers that they might like to have some day. Ask them to tell whether they think these jobs would be secure. Have students note the education or training they think they might need to get each job. Finally, have students note the wages they might expect to earn in each occupation. Students should summarize their findings in a short report.

Organizing Information

Have student pairs change all the headings in Chapter 9 of the Student Edition into questions. For example, the heading Supply, Demand, and Wages on page 114, can be rewritten as **How do supply and demand affect wages?** After pairs form questions, have them read the sections and then write a few sentences that answer each question.

Assessing Content Knowledge

Ask students to respond to the following questions. You may wish to encourage students with higher language proficiency to help beginning level students understand the questions.

Beginning Level Questions

Encourage students at this level to think about the answers to these questions and to offer short verbal responses.

1. Look at the Words to Know on page 113. What do businesses pay workers for their labor? (wages)

2. Read pages 116 and 117. Are wages generally higher or lower for workers with more skills and training? (higher)

3. Read page 117. True or false: The word *median* means that half the population earns more than the listed income, and half earns less. (true)

4. Look at the chart on page 117. What was the median income in 1998 for a man who was a high school graduate? ($31,477)

5. Look at the photograph on page 119. Are machines or humans building the cars? (machines)

Intermediate Level Questions

Encourage students at this level to offer verbal responses or short written responses to the following questions.

1. Read page 114. Who is included in the data gathered about the labor force in the United States? (Anyone over 16 who is employed or looking for work is in the labor force.)

2. Read page 114. How are wages determined? (by supply and demand)

3. Read page 115. Did the demand for autoworkers hold steady or fall when the demand for American cars fell? (The demand for autoworkers fell.)

4. Look at the Median Income chart on page 117. How do the incomes of men compare with those of women? (Men tend to earn more than women do, even when both have the same level of education.)

5. Read page 118. Do more productive workers usually earn less or more than other workers do? (They usually earn more.)

Advanced Level Questions

Encourage students at this level to provide written responses in complete sentences to the following questions.

1. Why should you be aware of changes in the economy? (If you are aware of changes in the economy, you can better ensure your chances of getting a job with good wages.)

2. Suppose people began to buy American cars in record numbers. What would probably happen to the demand for labor in auto factories? (The demand for labor in automobile factories would probably increase.)

3. How does finishing high school or going to college tend to help a worker? (Workers who finish high school or go to college tend to earn more.)

4. Why can productive businesses pay their workers higher wages? (Productive businesses earn more money.)

5. What is one advantage and one disadvantage of technology in the workplace? (Possible advantages—Technology increases productivity; technology creates new types of jobs. Possible disadvantage—Technology can eliminate the need for human labor.)

▶ Closing the Chapter

Distribute copies of the Spider Web found on page 54 of this guide. Students should use as a topic for the web **Workers and Wages**. Have students fill in each corner of the web with important facts, terms, and ideas from the chapter. When the web is completed, have students summarize the main ideas of the chapter.

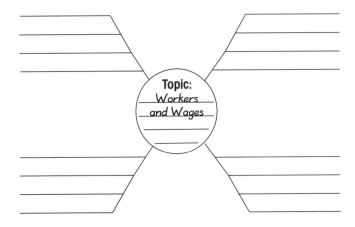

Topic: Workers and Wages

Chapter 10 Labor Unions pages 124–137

▶ Introducing the Chapter

Tapping Prior Knowledge

Distribute copies of the **KWL Chart** found on page 59 of this guide. Then, ask students whether they have relatives or friends who are members of labor unions. Ask them to share what they know about unions and to note this information in the **K** column of the chart. Then, encourage students to preview the chapter by reading the headings and by looking at the photographs and chart. While students preview, they can fill in the **W** column of the chart, noting what they want to learn about labor unions.

Preteaching Vocabulary

Personalizing Vocabulary Begin by asking students to preview the chapter for five unfamiliar words or phrases and to record them in their Word Logs. Ask students to use their bilingual dictionaries to define the words or phrases.

Identifying Essential Vocabulary Go over the pronunciation and meaning of each word or phrase in the box below. Then, ask students to work with a partner to write a sentence where they find the word or phrase in the chapter and then to replace the word or phrase with a familiar word or phrase.

Word or Phrase	Meaning
was sponsored by	was supported by (p. 126)
for only pennies a day	for very low wages (p. 126)
sweatshop	a factory with poor working conditions (p. 127)
kicked out onto the street	forced to leave (p. 127)
walk a picket line	walk in front of a workplace holding signs (p. 132)
put economic pressure on	lower income or revenue (p. 132)
displaced workers	workers who have lost their jobs (p. 134)

▶ Applying Content Knowledge

From the Chapter: Learn More About It: The AFL-CIO (page 135)

Ask students to read Learn More About It: The AFL-CIO on page 135 of the Student Edition. Point out that the feature notes that Samuel Gompers organized the AFL in 1886 and that John L. Lewis formed the CIO in 1938. The two organizations merged in 1955. Distribute copies of the Timeline found on page 63 of this guide. Ask students to begin a labor union timeline with these dates and facts. Then, as students read the chapter, have them add other events in the history of American labor unions.

Note Taking

Ask students to complete the KWL charts they began while they were previewing the chapter. Have students complete the **L** column of the chart once they have completed each section of the chapter. Encourage students to focus on the main ideas and most important terms from the chapter.

Personalizing the Lesson

Divide the class in half and conduct a debate on labor unions. One half of the class should argue why it is important for workers to join a union. The other half of the class should argue that unions are not good for workers. To help students get started, have them review the arguments given on pages 128 and 129 of the Student Edition. Encourage students to discuss ways in which union members, nonunion members, and management could conduct collective bargaining sessions in which an acceptable agreement for all could be reached over issues such as wages, hours, and benefits.

Organizing Information

Distribute copies of the Idea Web found on page 56 of this guide. As students read the chapter, ask them to fill in the idea web. Use the chapter title, **Labor Unions**, as the central topic. Place the headings **Types of Unions, Reasons for Unions, Reasons Against Unions**, and **Reasons for Declining Membership** in the outer shapes. Then, ask students to list key details that they learned about each heading.

Assessing Content Knowledge

Ask students to respond to the following questions. You may wish to encourage students with higher language proficiency to help beginning level students understand the questions.

Beginning Level Questions

Encourage students at this level to think about the answers to these questions and to offer short verbal responses.

1. Look at the photograph on page 124. What does the workers' sign say? (Jobs with Justice)

2. Look at the Words to Know on page 125. Is a strike or a boycott a work stoppage by labor? (a strike)

3. Read pages 128 and 129. True or false: Everyone believes that unions are necessary. (false)

4. Look at the photograph and caption on page 130. What are the workers doing? (striking)

5. Look at the chart on page 134. Which union had 760,000 members in 1999? (United Auto Workers)

Intermediate Level Questions

Encourage students at this level to offer verbal responses or short written responses to the following questions.

1. Read page 127. What was the name of the first large organization to fight for the eight-hour workday? (the National Labor Union)

2. Read pages 129 and 130. Does a union shop or an agency shop give workers the right not to join a union? (an agency shop)

3. Read page 131. What is collective bargaining? (labor unions and management working out an acceptable agreement)

4. Read page 132. How did the United Farm Workers win better wages and working conditions in the 1970s? (by encouraging a grape boycott)

5. Read page 133. Is union membership rising or falling in the United States? (falling)

Advanced Level Questions

Encourage students at this level to provide written responses in complete sentences to the following questions.

1. How did working conditions during the Industrial Revolution lead to the formation of the first union? (Because there was a large labor supply, businesses could afford to pay workers low wages. Workers believed that if they could join together, they could convince their managers to improve pay and working conditions.)

2. Why is it important to learn about unions whether you believe in them or not? (Labor unions are an important part of the U.S. economic system. Many workers belong to unions.)

3. In what situation do you not have to join a union? (If a state has a right-to-work law, then you have the right to work without joining a union or paying dues.)

4. Why is arbitration used to reach an agreement between unions and management? (An arbitrator is someone who does not have a personal interest in the outcome of the argument; therefore, he or she can determine a fair outcome.)

5. Why did unions lose membership in the latter part of the 1990s? (Unions lost membership because certain industries—such as the steel industry and many manufacturing industries—employ fewer workers. Foreign competition has also threatened job security, which gives unions less bargaining power than they once had. As a result, some people do not believe that unions can make a difference anymore.)

Closing the Chapter

Distribute copies of the Who, What, Why, Where, When, and How Chart found on page 61 of this guide. Ask students to work with a partner and complete a chart for the chapter. Students may wish to write **Who Formed Unions** underneath the word **Who** in the chart, **What Happened in Response to Unions** underneath the word **What** in the chart, and **Where Are Labor Unions Needed** underneath the word **Where** in the chart. They may wish to write **When Did Labor Unions First Organize** underneath the word **When** in the chart, **Why Did Labor Unions Organize** underneath the word **Why** in the chart, and **How Have Unions Changed the Workplace** underneath the word **How** in the chart. Have students complete the chart by reviewing the chapter. Then, have them write a summary about what they learned in the chapter.

Consumer Spending

pages 140–153

▶ Introducing the Chapter

Tapping Prior Knowledge

Ask students to recall a time when they saved up money to buy an item that was important to them. Have volunteers describe their experiences, including how they decided what to buy and where to buy it. Ask them if, looking back, they think they made a good spending decision.

Preteaching Vocabulary

Personalizing Vocabulary Have students form small groups. Have each group look for ten unfamiliar words or phrases from different sections of the chapter. Once groups have identified these words or phrases, ask them to record the words or phrases in their Word Logs and to use their bilingual dictionaries to define them. As a class, the groups may share their Word Logs.

Identifying Essential Vocabulary Go over the pronunciation and meaning of each word or phrase in the box below. Then, ask students to work with a partner to write the sentence where they find the word or phrase in the chapter and then to replace the word or phrase with a familiar word or phrase. Students may wish to consult their bilingual dictionaries as they rewrite the sentences.

Word or Phrase	Meaning
used public transportation	went by bus or train (p. 143)
a breakdown	a list of items (p. 143)
exclusive store	fashionable store (p. 145)
informed decision	decision based on information (p. 147)
outlined in a speech	discussed in a speech (p. 148)
honor the warranty	to do what the warranty says (p. 148)
bewildered	confused (p. 148)

▶ Applying Content Knowledge

From the Chapter: Budget Chart (page 144)

Ask students to look at Megan's monthly budget on page 144 of the Student Edition. Have them discuss the items on which she spends her money. Then, have students make up an original budget. They might show how they spend the money they typically earn at part-time jobs, or they could show an approximate budget for their own families. Students might also make up an ideal budget, listing how much they plan to earn and spend once they enter the work force full time.

Organizing Information

Distribute copies of the Sequence of Events Chart on page 53 of this guide. Ask students to entitle the chart **Making Good Spending Decisions**. Then, have them label the first three numbered boxes **Step 1: Set Goals**, **Step 2: Gather Information**, and **Step 3: Think About the Trade-offs**. Students should review facts and ideas from pages 143–147 to list important details about each step for making sound spending decisions. Finally, have students summarize their chart in a short paragraph.

Role-Playing

Divide the class into pairs. Ask pairs of students to role-play a situation in which they are shopping for an expensive item that they have saved for, such as a bike, a prom dress, or a graduation ring. One student can role-play the consumer while the other plays a salesperson. Have students playing the consumer ask questions that show they have set goals, gathered information, and thought about the trade-offs. After role-playing, have students discuss their experiences with the whole class.

Assessing Content Knowledge

Ask students to respond to the following questions. You may wish to encourage students with higher language proficiency to help beginning level students understand the questions.

Beginning Level Questions

Encourage students at this level to think about the answers to these questions and to offer short verbal responses.

1. Read the Words to Know on page 141. Does a limited warranty or a full warranty promise to repair or replace all parts at no cost? (a full warranty)

2. Look at the bottom of page 142. What is the first step for making a sound decision about what to buy? (Set goals.)

3. Look at Megan's budget at the top of page 144. How much income does Megan have left after paying all her expenses each month? ($300)

4. Look at the heading near the bottom of page 146. Should you think about the trade-off before you buy something? (yes)

5. Look at the table on page 149. Name one government agency to contact with a consumer complaint. (Possible answer: Auto Safety Hotline)

Intermediate Level Questions

Encourage students at this level to offer verbal responses or short written responses to the following questions.

1. Read page 142. What are the three steps for making sound spending decisions? (Set goals; gather information; think about the trade-offs.)

2. Read page 143. How do you determine how much money you have left in your budget to spend on nonnecessities? (Subtract what you spend on necessities from your income.)

3. Read page 144. What are you doing when you compare the price, quality, and features of similar products? (comparison shopping)

4. Read pages 145 and 146. What are two questions to ask when gathering information about a product? (Possible answers: Does the product have a written warranty? What kind of name does the product have? Where are you shopping? What additional costs will there be?)

5. Read page 148. Where should you look in the phone book if you are seeking consumer protection? (Under Consumer Protection Organizations)

Advanced Level Questions

Encourage students at this level to provide written responses in complete sentences to the following questions.

1. Why do consumers have to make choices about spending decisions? (Consumers have limited income.)

2. Suppose you have set spending goals and have the money to buy something. What is the next step in making a spending decision? (The next step is to gather information about a product.)

3. Why is it important to get a warranty on a product you might buy? (The warranty protects you if the product does not work the way it should.)

4. How does Megan's list on page 147 help her decide which car to buy? (The list shows exactly what she is getting and giving up with each car.)

5. What are some rights that consumers have? (Possible answers: Consumers have the right to choose among different products; they have a right to safe products; they have the right to be fully informed about products they buy.)

Closing the Chapter

Distribute copies of the Two-Column Chart found on page 50 of this guide. Have students write **Consumer Spending** as the topic and label the columns **Question** and **Answer**. Next, have them list the questions in the left column as shown on the chart below. Then, have students fill in the answers to their questions in the right column.

Topic: Consumer Spending

Question	Answer
Why is it important to set spending goals?	
How can you gather information about a product?	
What does "think about the trade-offs" mean?	
Who protects consumers?	

Chapter 12 · Saving and Borrowing

pages 154–165

▶ Introducing the Chapter

Tapping Prior Knowledge

Ask students to share how they save their money and why. If students have bank accounts, ask them to tell how they opened these accounts and how the accounts work. Discuss why most people keep their money in a bank rather than at home. You might also ask students why they might like to have their own credit cards some day. Then, have students preview the chapter by reading the headings and subheadings. After previewing, ask students to predict how the information in the chapter might be helpful to them.

Preteaching Vocabulary

Personalizing Vocabulary Begin by asking students to preview the chapter for five unfamiliar words or phrases and to record them in their Word Logs. Ask students to use their bilingual dictionaries to define the words or phrases. Students may form small groups to share their Word Logs.

Identifying Essential Vocabulary Go over the pronunciation and meaning of each phrase in the box below. Then, ask students to work in pairs to write a sentence for each phrase.

Word or Phrase	Meaning
in the long run	in the future (p. 155)
put away money	save money (p. 156)
stash their savings	hide their savings (p. 157)
the interest mounts	the interest increases (p. 161)
a running total	an up-to-date amount (p. 161)
sign on the dotted line	agree to a loan or deal by signing your name (p. 162)
face value	the amount printed on the front of the bond (p. 163)

▶ Applying Content Knowledge

From the Chapter: Learn More About It: U.S. Savings Bonds (page 163)

Ask students to read aloud Learn More About It: U.S. Savings Bonds on page 163 of the Student Edition. Then, have students stop by the office of a local bank or go online to get more information about these bonds. At the same time, students can pick up brochures about other savings plans that the bank offers. Have students read and discuss these brochures in small groups.

Organizing Information

Distribute copies of the Three-Column Chart found on page 51 of this guide. Ask students to label the headings **Type of Savings or Borrowing Account, Pros,** and **Cons.** In the first column, have students list the following types of savings or borrowing accounts: **Regular Savings Account, Money Market Account, CD, Credit Card, Bank Loan,** and **Government Bond.** Then, have them summarize the main ideas of the chapter by listing some pros and cons of each type of savings or borrowing account.

Using Realia

Ask students to take a close look at the advertising letters that banks send to consumers to persuade them to open credit-card accounts. Have students find and read the "fine print" in these advertising letters. Then, ask them to list the benefits and possible dangers of owning a credit card. Students may wish to review pages 161 and 162 of the Student Edition for help with this exercise.

Assessing Content Knowledge

Ask students to respond to the following questions. You may wish to encourage students with higher language proficiency to help beginning level students understand the questions.

Beginning Level Questions

Encourage students at this level to think about the answers to these questions and to offer short verbal responses.

1. Look at the Words to Know on page 155. Is principal or collateral the original amount of money borrowed in a loan? (principal)

2. Look at the photograph and caption on page 156. What do people save for in order to buy a house? (a down payment)

3. Look at page 157. Where can you get savings accounts? (at financial institutions)

4. Look at the chart on page 159. How many types of savings accounts are being compared? (three)

5. Look at page 161. What does APR mean? (annual percentage rate)

Intermediate Level Questions

Encourage students at this level to offer verbal responses or short written responses to the following questions.

1. Read pages 156 and 157. Why do people save their money? (Possible answers: to buy a large purchase; for emergencies; for future spending, such as retirement or college; to give a sense of security)

2. Read pages 157–159. What are two questions you should ask when shopping for a savings account? (Possible answers: How much interest does the account pay? Is there a minimum deposit? Is it a time-deposit account? Are there any related fees?)

3. Look at the chart on page 159. Which type of account usually pays the highest interest rate? (a certificate of deposit)

4. Read pages 161 and 162. What are two key things to look for when getting a credit card? (Possible answers: the annual percentage rate, membership fees, service or transaction fees)

5. Read page 162. What do banks often need from you before they will approve your loan? (Possible answers: to fill out forms, proof that loan payments can be made, collateral)

Advanced Level Questions

Encourage students at this level to provide written responses in complete sentences to the following questions.

1. Why is saving good for the U.S. economy? (The money that consumers save can be loaned to businesses to help them grow.)

2. Why might it be a bad idea to keep your savings as cash at home? (You will not earn any interest on cash that you do not deposit in a savings account.)

3. Why might people *not* want to put their money in a time-deposit account, even if it pays a higher interest than other accounts? (Money must be left in a time-deposit account for a fixed time. Taking money out before that time will result in a penalty, often losing the interest made on the money. Some people might feel they cannot commit their money for a long time.)

4. Why do people often need to borrow money? (Their savings and income are not enough to meet their needs and wants.)

5. Why are credit cards sometimes dangerous? (People are tempted to charge more than they can afford. Then, they are charged a high interest for the amount they cannot pay.)

Closing the Chapter

Distribute copies of the Four-Column Chart found on page 52 of this guide. Ask students to title the chart **Types of Savings Accounts** and to label the columns **Regular Savings Accounts, U.S. Savings Bonds, Money Market Accounts,** and **Certificates of Deposit.** Ask students to complete the chart by filling in the main idea and details about each type of savings account using information from the chapter. Then, have students record the similarities and differences between the four types of saving accounts in a short summary.

Topic: Types of Savings Accounts

Regular Savings Accounts	U.S. Savings Bonds	Money Market Accounts	Certificates of Deposit

Chapter 13 Money

pages 168–179

Introducing the Chapter

Tapping Prior Knowledge

Display a U.S. dollar bill to the class. Ask students, *Why do people accept this printed paper for goods and services? From where does money come? Is money essential for today's economy? How so?* Ask students to preview the chapter by reading the headings and subheadings. Then, have students predict what they will learn in the chapter.

Preteaching Vocabulary

Personalizing Vocabulary Begin by asking students to preview the chapter for five unfamiliar words or phrases and to record them in their Word Logs. Ask students to use their bilingual dictionaries to define the words or phrases. Students may form small groups to share their Word Logs.

Identifying Essential Vocabulary Go over the pronunciation and meaning of each word or phrase in the box below. Then, ask each student to write a sentence for each word or phrase. Ask students to rewrite their sentences, leaving a blank space in place of the vocabulary term. Have students trade sentences with a partner and fill in the blanks in the sentences their partner wrote.

Word or Phrase	Meaning
the arrangement	the agreement (p. 169)
specialize	to train oneself in one activity or study (p. 173)
pinch off	break off (p. 174)
insulate	cover (p. 174)

Applying Content Knowledge

From the Chapter: Learn More About It: New Currency (page 177)

Ask students to read Learn More About It: New Currency on page 177 of the Student Edition. Then, ask students to conduct additional research on U.S. money. Students may draw facts by looking through the chapter and by looking closely at the coins and bills in their home. They also may do research in the library or on the Internet. Have students illustrate their money facts on posterboard. Compile students' work and display it in the classroom.

Role-Playing

Ask students to role-play a bartering session in which they try to arrange an actual trade of real items. Then, have students compare this bartering session to buying the goods with money. Ask them to make a chart that lists some of the pros and cons of both bartering and using money.

Organizing Information

Distribute copies of the Idea Web found on page 56 of this guide. The central topic of the web should be **What Money Should Be.** The five shapes surrounding the central topic should be labeled **Widely Accepted and Recognized, Scarce, Easily Divided, Durable,** and **Portable.** As students read the chapter, have them complete the web with ideas and details about the five desirable qualities of money. Students should pay particular attention to pages 173–175 in the Student Edition.

Personalizing the Lesson

Ask students to design their own money, including a paper bill and a coin. Have students present their currency to the class. Presentations should include information on why students think their bills and coins illustrate the desirable qualities of money and why their currency would make a welcome addition to the U.S. money supply.

Assessing Content Knowledge

Ask students to respond to the following questions. You may wish to encourage students with higher language proficiency to help beginning level students understand the questions.

Beginning Level Questions
Encourage students at this level to think about the answers to these questions and to offer short verbal responses.

1. Look at the photograph on page 168. What machine can you see? (an ATM)
2. Look at the Words to Know on page 169. Is currency both coins and paper money? (yes)
3. Look at the photograph on page 170. What are the boys bartering? (baseball cards)
4. Read pages 173–175. In how many ways is all money alike? (five)
5. Look at the table on page 176. Did people always use paper bills for money? (no)

Intermediate Level Questions
Encourage students at this level to offer verbal responses or short written responses to the following questions.

1. Read page 171. What is bartering? (Bartering is the direct trade of one good or service for another without the use of money.)
2. Read page 173. How does money allow people to specialize? (Money helps free up time from making food, shelter, and clothing. Therefore, people can take their time and train in services for others, such as teaching.)
3. Read pages 173–175. What are two desirable qualities for money? (Possible answers: The money should be widely accepted and recognized; the money should be scarce; the money should be easily divided; the money should be durable; the money should be portable.)
4. Read page 175. In addition to coins and paper bills, what makes up our country's money supply? (demand deposit accounts)
5. Look at the table on page 176. Which country once used tea as money? (China)

Advanced Level Questions
Encourage students at this level to provide written responses in complete sentences to the following questions.

1. What are some problems with bartering? (People might not have the things you want to barter for; the things you want to barter might spoil if you don't trade them right away.)
2. What are some advantages of using money? (Everyone will accept money for goods and services; money compares the value of goods and services; money helps us know what something is worth; money is a way to store value.)
3. What would happen if a country's money was not scarce? (The money would be less valuable and buy fewer goods and services.)
4. Why are added security features needed on today's money? (The features make the money more difficult to counterfeit.)
5. Why are demand deposit accounts considered part of the money supply? (Banks must supply people cash from these accounts upon request.)

Closing the Chapter

Distribute copies of the Outline found on page 55 of this guide. Ask students to use the headings and information from the chapter to complete the outline. Then, have students use the completed outline to write a summary of what they learned in the chapter.

Topic: Money
I. Bartering vs. Money
   A. _____
   B. _____
   C. _____
II. Specialization and Money
   A. _____
   B. _____
III. What Are Desirable Qualities for Money?
   A. _____
   B. _____
   C. _____
   D. _____
   E. _____
IV. Today's Money Supply
   A. _____
   B. _____

Chapter 14

Banks and the Federal Reserve System

pages 180–189

▶ Introducing the Chapter

Tapping Prior Knowledge

Ask students if any of them has ever toured a bank. What did they see? Next, have students look at the photograph and caption of the bank panic on page 180 of the Student Edition. Ask students, *Are the banks in your community a safe place to keep money? What makes you feel that way?* Then, ask students to preview the chapter by reading the Words to Know on page 181 of the Student Edition and the headings of the chapter. Finally, have students make predictions on what they might learn in the chapter.

Preteaching Vocabulary

Personalizing Vocabulary Have students form small groups. Have each group look for ten unfamiliar words or phrases from different sections of the chapter. Ask students to record the words or phrases in their Word Logs and to use their bilingual dictionaries to define the words or phrases. As a class, the groups may share their Word Logs.

Identifying Essential Vocabulary Go over the pronunciation and meaning of each word or phrase in the box below. Then, distribute an index card to each student. Ask each student to write a question on the index card using one or more of the vocabulary terms. Then, have students exchange cards with a partner and answer their partner's question.

Word or Phrase	Meaning
spring crops	crops planted in spring (p. 181)
closed its doors	stopped doing business (p. 182)
lose confidence in	no longer think safe (p. 182)
cash on hand	cash that is not invested (p. 182)
to back up their deposits	to cover their deposits (p. 183)

▶ Applying Content Knowledge

From the Chapter: Learn More About It: The FDIC (page 187)

Ask students to read Learn More About It: The FDIC on page 187 of the Student Edition. Ask students, *What is the Federal Deposit Insurance Corporation?* Encourage students to use their bilingual dictionaries to help in answering the question. Work with students to help them understand the difference between the FDIC and the Federal Reserve System.

Using Visuals

Ask students to look at the map of the Federal Reserve System on page 183 of the Student Edition. Have students create a chart from the information on the map with the headings labeled 1 to 12 for each Federal Reserve District. Under each heading, have students list which states are found in each of the 12 districts. Some states are in more than one district. Students should consult a map of the United States for help with this step. Then, have students make symbols for a Federal Reserve Bank City and a Board of Governors City. Ask students to mark that symbol next to the appropriate states on their charts. Students may also wish to visit the San Francisco Federal Reserve Bank Web site at www.frbsf.org to learn more about the Federal Reserve System.

Organizing Information

Distribute copies of the Three-Column Chart found on page 51 of this guide. Have students entitle the chart **Types of Banks.** Ask students to label the columns **Federal Reserve Bank, Commercial Bank,** and **Credit Union.** As students read the chapter, ask them to fill in details that describe each type of bank. Then, have students write a summary of the differences and similarities between the types of banks in a short paragraph.

Assessing Content Knowledge

Ask students to respond to the following questions. You may wish to encourage students with higher language proficiency to help beginning level students understand the questions.

Beginning Level Questions

Encourage students at this level to think about the answers to these questions and to offer short verbal responses.

1. Look at the Words to Know on page 181. Do members who belong to a certain group own a credit union or a commercial bank? (a credit union)

2. Read page 182. True or false: The Federal Reserve System is the name of the central bank of the United States. (true)

3. Look at the map and caption on page 183. How many districts is the Federal Reserve System divided into? (12)

4. Look at the twenty-dollar bill and caption on page 184. Do the letters and numbers on your bills tell you which Federal Reserve Bank distributed them? (yes)

5. Read the heading on page 185. Are there other types of banks besides the Federal Reserve Bank? (yes)

Intermediate Level Questions

Encourage students at this level to offer verbal responses or short written responses to the following questions.

1. Read pages 181 and 182. What is it called when everyone tries to withdraw their money from a bank at once? (a bank panic)

2. Read pages 182 and 183. Do individuals or other banks have accounts with the Fed? (other banks)

3. Read page 184. What does the "L12" on the photograph of the twenty-dollar bill stand for? (the Federal Reserve bank that distributed the bill—San Francisco)

4. Read pages 185 and 186. What are two types of banks that are not part of the Federal Reserve System? (commercial banks and credit unions)

5. Read the last paragraph on page 186. What is one thing you should consider when choosing a bank? (Possible answers: the interest rate on a savings account; the interest rate charged on a loan; the fees charged to open a checking account; location; service)

Advanced Level Questions

Encourage students at this level to provide written responses in complete sentences to the following questions.

1. Why can a bank fail during a bank panic? (People rush to withdraw all their money from a bank, and the bank does not have all the money on hand to redistribute because it has lent some of it out.)

2. What is check clearing? (Check clearing is the way the Fed transfers checks and money between different banks.)

3. How does the Federal Reserve affect the country's money supply? (It can encourage or discourage people from making loans.)

4. Why might people who work for the same company or are in the same group form a credit union? (They might be able to offer themselves banking services at a lower cost than commercial banks can.)

5. Why can most people in the United States feel that their savings accounts in banks are safe? (The FDIC insures bank deposits up to $100,000 and will pay people their money back if the bank fails.)

Closing the Chapter

Distribute copies of the Spider Web found on page 54 of this guide. The central topic of the web should read **The Banking System.** The outer corners of the web should be labeled **Federal Reserve Bank, Credit Unions, Commercial Banks,** and the **Federal Deposit Insurance Corporation.** As students read the chapter, have them complete the web with ideas and details about the banking system. When the web is completed, have students use it to write a summary of what they learned in the chapter.

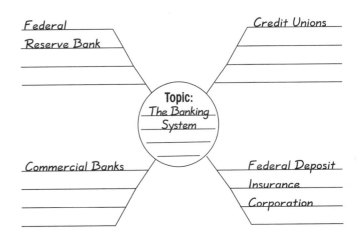

Chapter 15
Gross Domestic Product

pages 192–203

▶ Introducing the Chapter

Tapping Prior Knowledge

Ask students if they have ever stood in line to buy an item such as tickets to see a ballgame. Then, have students look at the photograph and caption on page 201 of the Student Edition. Have students explain the difference between standing in line waiting to buy tickets to an event and standing in line to buy a needed good such as bread.

Preteaching Vocabulary

Personalizing Vocabulary Have students form small groups. Have each group look for ten unfamiliar words or phrases from different sections of the chapter. Ask students to record the words or phrases in their Word Logs and to use their bilingual dictionaries to define the words or phrases. As a class, the groups may share their Word Logs.

Identifying Essential Vocabulary Go over the pronunciation and meaning of each phrase in the box below. Then, ask students to work in pairs to write the sentence where they find the phrase in the chapter and then to replace the phrase with a familiar phrase.

Word or Phrase	Meaning
overall health	health as a whole (p. 193)
the real lesson	the most important points (p. 194)
well off	comfortable financially (p. 196)
a turning point	the moment when things change direction (p. 198)

▶ Applying Content Knowledge

From the Chapter: The Changing Economic World: The Great Depression (page 200)

Ask students to read The Changing Economic World: The Great Depression on page 200 of the Student Edition. Have students research more information about this significant event in the history of the U.S. economy. Discuss the photograph on page 201 of the Student Edition with students. Then, ask students to find other period photographs that show the poverty and despair of the Great Depression. Have students prepare a short presentation of their photographs, including a few sentences about each one that explains what is taking place and how the U.S. government attempted to deal with the problem.

Organizing Information

Distribute copies of the Sequence of Events Chart found on page 53 of this guide. Have students read pages 197–199 of the Student Edition. Then, ask them to entitle the chart **The Business Cycle** and to label each box as follows: **1. The GDP Increases, 2. The Economy Expands, 3. The Economy Reaches a Peak, 4. The Economy Contracts, 5. The GDP Decreases,** and **6. The Economy Reaches a Trough.** Then, have students write a sentence or two about each stage of the business cycle. After the chart is completed, have students write a summary of what they have learned.

Personalizing the Lesson

Ask students to discuss how the business cycle, with its ups and downs, affects families and communities. Students might draw on the experiences of people they know. Then, have students tell what they might do to protect themselves from the hardships caused by contracting economic activity.

▶ Assessing Content Knowledge

Ask students to respond to the following questions. You may wish to encourage students with higher language proficiency to help beginning level students understand the questions.

Beginning Level Questions

Encourage students at this level to think about the answers to these questions and to offer short verbal responses.

1. Look at the Words to Know on page 193. What is the abbreviation for Gross Domestic Product? (GDP)

2. Read the caption for the photograph on page 194. True or false: Bread is a final good because consumers do not plan to re-sell it to others. (true)

3. Read pages 195 and 196. Is there a difference between GDP and real GDP? (yes)

4. Look at Graph 15.1 on page 197. Did real GDP go up or down between 1970 and 2000? (up)

5. Look at Graph 15.2 on page 198. What is it an example of? (a business cycle)

Intermediate Level Questions

Encourage students at this level to offer verbal responses or short written responses to the following questions.

1. Look at the Words to Know on page 193. What is a recession? (a time period when GDP decreases for two quarters [six months] in a row)

2. Read page 196. When does inflation occur? (when the average price of all goods and services goes up)

3. Look at Graph 15.1 on page 197. What was our country's real GDP in 1992? (almost 5 trillion dollars)

4. Read page 198. Does the economy make fewer goods during an expansion? (no)

5. Look at Graph 15.2 on page 198. Does the GDP fall after a peak in the business cycle? (yes)

Advanced Level Questions

Encourage students at this level to provide written responses in complete sentences to the following questions.

1. Why do economists measure the GDP of the country? (The GDP is a good way to determine the overall health of the economy.)

2. How is real GDP different from GDP? (The real GDP measures real increases in production by subtracting the effects of inflation.)

3. Look at Graph 15.1 on page 197. How did the GDP of the United States change between 1970 and 2000? (The GDP more than doubled from almost 3 trillion to almost 7.5 trillion dollars.)

4. Look at Graph 15.2 on page 198. At which point in the business cycle would GDP be highest? (GDP would be highest at the peak of the business cycle.)

5. How is a depression different from a recession? (A depression is an extremely bad recession that lasts a long time.)

▶ Closing the Chapter

Distribute copies of the Outline found on page 55 of this guide. Students should write in the main heads and subheads as shown below first. Then, ask students to use the information from the chapter to complete the outline. Once the outline is completed, ask students to use it to summarize what they learned in the chapter.

> **Topic: The Health of the Economy**
> I. Gross Domestic Product
>   A. Inflation
>   1. _____
>   2. _____
>   B. Real GDP
>   1. _____
>   2. _____
> II. The Business Cycle
>   A. Expansion
>   1. _____
>   2. _____
>   B. Contraction
>   1. _____
>   2. _____
>   C. Recession
>   1. _____
>   2. _____

Chapter 16 — Inflation

▶ Introducing the Chapter

Tapping Prior Knowledge
Demonstrate the meaning of inflation by blowing up a balloon and making the connection that the same small balloon gets bigger and bigger with inflation. Ask students if they have ever noticed that the prices of things they buy go up. Their parents or other adults may sometimes talk about how much less some products cost years ago. Ask students to make a general statement about how prices have changed over the last 70 years or more.

Preteaching Vocabulary
Personalizing Vocabulary Begin by asking students to preview the chapter for five unfamiliar words or phrases and to record them in their Word Logs. Ask students to use their bilingual dictionaries to define the words or phrases. Students may form small groups to share their Word Logs.

Identifying Essential Vocabulary Go over the pronunciation and meaning of each phrase in the box below. Then, ask students to work with a partner to write the sentence where they find the phrase in the chapter and then to replace the phrase with a familiar word or phrase. Students may wish to consult their bilingual dictionaries as they rewrite the sentences.

Word or Phrase	Meaning
no laughing matter	serious, not funny (p. 206)
compiled monthly	put together every month (p. 206)
fast and furious	out of control (p. 208)
has jumped	has increased in price (p. 208)
highly desirable	very attractive (p. 209)
keep in check	control (p. 210)

▶ Applying Content Knowledge

From the Chapter: You Decide (pages 208 and 211)
Divide the class into small groups. Ask students to read the You Decide features on pages 208 and 211 of the Student Edition. Have the groups discuss the questions based on what they have read in the chapter. Have volunteers tell their answers to the class. Then, ask students some additional You Decide questions, such as *Should the government control prices to limit inflation? Is deflation good for the economy since it helps people afford more goods?* Once each group comes to a consensus about the questions, ask a spokesperson from each group to write that group's answers on the board.

Organizing Information
Distribute copies of the Two-Column Chart found on page 50 of this guide. Have students entitle the chart **Inflation**. Ask students to label the columns **Cause** and **Effect**. In the Effect column, have students list **Demand-pull inflation** and **Cost-push inflation**. Then, have them write the cause of each type of inflation in the Cause column. After completing the charts, ask volunteers to describe situations that cause each type of inflation.

Personalizing the Lesson
Ask students to look at the Consumer Price Index table on page 207 of the Student Edition. Have them pick a year from the table. Then, tell them to suppose that they are urban consumers from the past. Have students figure out how much typical items—such as food, clothing, and transportation—would have cost in the year they picked. Finally, have them design a poster that shows these items and their prices. For example, if a student picks 1960, then that student's poster would show items that cost on average less than 30 percent of what they do now.

▶ Assessing Content Knowledge

Ask students to respond to the following questions. You may wish to encourage students with higher language proficiency to help beginning level students understand the questions.

Beginning Level Questions

Encourage students at this level to think about the answers to these questions and to offer short verbal responses.

1. Look at the photograph and caption on page 204. How much did a movie ticket cost in 1930? (70 cents)

2. Read the Words to Know on page 205. What kind of inflation is caused by the rising cost of resources? (cost-push inflation)

3. Read the Words to Know on page 205. What is a decrease in the average price of goods called? (deflation)

4. Read page 206. Is inflation an increase in the average price of goods and services? (yes)

5. Look at the table on page 207. What was the Consumer Price Index in 1991? (136.2)

Intermediate Level Questions

Encourage students at this level to offer verbal responses or short written responses to the following questions.

1. Read page 206. What index measures inflation? (the Consumer Price Index)

2. Look at the table on page 207. Did the Consumer Price Index go up or down over time? (up)

3. Read page 208. True or false: Inflation is always a slow and gradual increase in prices. (false)

4. Read pages 209 and 210. What is caused by too many dollars chasing too few goods? (demand-pull inflation)

5. Read page 210. Does a rise or a drop in the prices of resources cause inflation? (a rise)

Advanced Level Questions

Encourage students at this level to provide written responses in complete sentences to the following questions.

1. What happens during times of deflation? (Prices of goods on average go down during times of deflation.)

2. What does the Consumer Price Index show? (The Consumer Price Index, or CPI, shows how prices have changed over time. It is a way to measure inflation.)

3. What is a cost-of-living increase? (A cost-of-living increase is a raise given to a worker to allow the worker to buy the same amount of goods and services despite inflation.)

4. What causes demand-pull inflation? (Demand-pull inflation occurs when consumers spend their money faster than producers increase production.)

5. What causes cost-push inflation? (Cost-push inflation occurs when the prices of important resources rise.)

▶ Closing the Chapter

Distribute copies of the Spider Web found on page 54 of this guide. Ask students to label the central topic **Inflation** and the corners **Causes of Inflation, Effects of Inflation, Consumer Price Index,** and **Hyperinflation.** As students review the chapter, have them fill in information about each of the terms in the corners of the web. Then, have students use the completed web to create a summary of what they learned in the chapter.

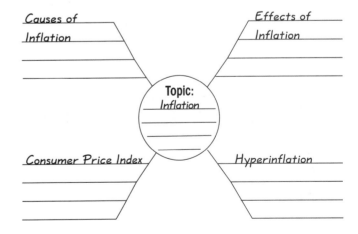

Unemployment

pages 214–225

Introducing the Chapter

Tapping Prior Knowledge

Write the word *unemployment* on the board. Circle the prefix *un-*, which means "not," and the suffix *–ment*, which means "the state of." Elicit that *unemployment* means "the state of not being employed." Ask students, *Why is unemployment a problem for workers and their families?* Then, have students preview the chapter by reading the headings and by looking at the table on page 216 of the Student Edition. Finally, ask volunteers to suggest why a high unemployment rate is not only a problem for the workers (and their families) who are out of work but for the economy as a whole.

Preteaching Vocabulary

Personalizing Vocabulary Have students form small groups. Have each group look for ten unfamiliar words or phrases from different sections of the chapter. Once groups have identified these words or phrases, ask them to record the words or phrases in their Word Logs and to use their bilingual dictionaries to define them.

Identifying Essential Vocabulary Go over the pronunciation and meaning of each phrase in the box below. Then, distribute an index card to each student. Ask students to write a question on the index card using one or more of the vocabulary terms. Then, have students exchange cards with a partner and answer their partner's question.

Word or Phrase	Meaning
laid off	lost a job (p. 215)
times will get tough	the economy will weaken (p. 217)
the off season	the season when there is no work (p. 218)
a booming Sunbelt city	a city in the southwest United States with a fast-growing economy (p. 221)
a few openings	a few jobs that are not filled (p. 221)
great strides to be made	much progress to make (p. 221)

Applying Content Knowledge

From the Chapter: Table (page 216)

Ask students to look at the table that shows the U.S. unemployment rate between 1920 and 1997 on page 216 of the Student Edition. Then, ask students to do online or magazine research to find out about the unemployment rate in the United States since 1997. Suggest that students make a table that shows the rate for four recent years, similar to the one on page 216. Finally, ask students to draw conclusions about the U.S. economy based on the number of people looking for work in those years.

Role-Playing

Invite groups of students to role-play a conversation that unemployed workers might have at a local employment office. Ask each student to choose one of the types of unemployment described in the chapter. As the students talk, ask them to discuss the different reasons for why they are unemployed and what they hope to do about finding new jobs.

Note Taking

Have students copy the following questions into their notebooks. **How does the U.S. government measure the unemployment rate? What are four causes of unemployment? How does employment vary among different groups? What is unemployment insurance?** As students read Chapter 17 of the Student Edition, have them answer each question. Finally, have students form small groups to compare their answers to the questions.

Summarizing

Ask students to work in pairs to read and answer the Check Your Understanding questions on pages 217 and 220 of the Student Edition. Suggest that students alternate reading and answering the questions. Students may use their answers to write a summary of the main ideas of the chapter.

Assessing Content Knowledge

Ask students to respond to the following questions. You may wish to encourage students with higher language proficiency to help beginning level students understand the questions.

Beginning Level Questions

Encourage students at this level to think about the answers to these questions and to offer short verbal responses.

1. Look at page 214. What is the woman in the photograph doing? (looking for a job)

2. Look at the Words to Know on page 215. What do we call the percentage of people in the labor force who cannot find jobs? (the unemployment rate)

3. Look at the table on page 216. Does the unemployment rate change for each year shown on the table? (yes)

4. Read page 217. Are changes in the business cycle a cause of unemployment? (yes)

5. Read pages 220 and 221. Does the unemployment rate vary from place to place? (yes)

Intermediate Level Questions

Encourage students at this level to offer verbal responses or short written responses to the following questions.

1. Look at the table on page 216. What was the unemployment rate in the United States in 1976? (7.7%)

2. Read page 217. When does cyclical unemployment occur? (when production decreases in the business cycle)

3. Read page 218. What kind of unemployment might be caused by bad weather? (seasonal unemployment)

4. Read page 220. What goal does government have for the unemployed? (Possible answers: to have enough jobs for everybody who wants to work; temporarily unemployed people should be able to find work quickly.)

5. Read page 221. Which two groups of people are often hit hardest by unemployment? (the young and minorities)

Advanced Level Questions

Encourage students at this level to provide written responses in complete sentences to the following questions.

1. What people make up the labor force? (The labor force is made up of people over 16 who have jobs or are looking for work.)

2. Why does unemployment go up after a peak in the business cycle? (When production begins to shrink, businesses need fewer workers.)

3. How can structural unemployment be lowered? (It can be lowered through further education and training.)

4. What causes frictional unemployment? (Frictional unemployment occurs when people voluntarily quit to find new jobs.)

5. Why will there always be some unfilled jobs in a free society, such as that of the United States? (People can choose their jobs and are free to quit jobs and look for new ones at any time.)

Closing the Chapter

Distribute copies of the Four-Column Chart found on page 52 of this guide. Have students entitle the chart **Types of Unemployment** and label the four columns **Cyclical Unemployment**, **Seasonal Unemployment**, **Structural Unemployment**, and **Frictional Unemployment**. Then, ask them to fill in details about each cause of unemployment. When possible, ask students to give examples of workers who are unemployed by each cause.

Topic: Types of Unemployment

Cyclical Unemployment	Seasonal Unemployment	Structural Unemployment	Frictional Unemployment

Chapter 18 ▷ The Problem of Poverty

▶ Introducing the Chapter

Tapping Prior Knowledge

Write the word *poverty* on the board. Next, distribute copies of the **KWL** Chart found on page 59 of this guide. Have students note what they already know about poverty in the **K** column of the chart. Then, ask students to think about what they want to learn about poverty in the **W** column of the chart. Finally, ask students, *What are some problems and difficulties that people in poverty might face? What might a person living in poverty do to get help?*

Preteaching Vocabulary

Personalizing Vocabulary Begin by asking students to preview the chapter for five unfamiliar words or phrases and to record them in their Word Logs. Ask students to use their bilingual dictionaries to define the words or phrases.

Identifying Essential Vocabulary Go over the pronunciation and meaning of each word or phrase in the box below. Then, ask each student to write a sentence for each word or phrase. Ask students to rewrite their sentences, leaving a blank space in place of the vocabulary term. Have students trade sentences with a partner and fill in the blanks in the sentences their partner wrote.

Word or Phrase	Meaning
armed itself with tax dollars	fought with money raised by taxes (p. 227)
threshold	the point where something begins (p. 228)
to make ends meet	to pay their bills (p. 229)
nonprofit organizations	organizations that are focused on helping people, not on earning profits (p. 231)
charitable organizations	organizations whose goals include providing funds, services, and aid to certain people (p. 231)
federal funding	money from the federal government (p. 232)
more perplexing	harder to understand (p. 236)

▶ Applying Content Knowledge

From the Chapter: Economics Facts (pages 231 and 234)

Ask students to read the Economics Facts given on pages 231 and 234 of the Student Edition. Then, as they read the chapter, ask them to write original Economics Facts about poverty and the government's efforts to eradicate the problem. Each Economics Fact should be at least two sentences. Students may print each fact on a sheet of paper, add illustrations, and compile the facts in a booklet.

Note Taking

Ask students to look again at the KWL charts they began while previewing the chapter. Ask them to review what they noted in the **K** and **W** columns. Then, have students discuss whether the chapter answered their questions. Finally, have students complete the **L** column by listing some of the main ideas of the chapter.

Summarizing

Ask students to work in pairs to read and answer the Check Your Understanding questions on pages 229, 230, 234, and 235 of the Student Edition. Suggest that students alternate reading and answering the questions. Have students use their answers to write two or more paragraphs that summarize the chapter. Students may use their summaries to review Chapter 18 of the Student Edition.

Personalizing the Lesson

Tell students that they are among the top advisors of the President of the United States. Like President Johnson in the 1960s, their task is to come up with a way to lift people in the United States above the poverty line. Divide the class into smaller groups to discuss what they would do to achieve this goal. Then, have each group list five or more major steps they would take to raise incomes dramatically.

Assessing Content Knowledge

Ask students to respond to the following questions. You may wish to encourage students with higher language proficiency to help beginning level students understand the questions.

Beginning Level Questions

Encourage students at this level to think about the answers to these questions and to offer short verbal responses.

1. Read page 227. Which President of the United States declared a war on poverty in the 1960s? (President Lyndon Johnson)

2. Read page 228. Is the poverty line a way to measure who lives in poverty? (yes)

3. Read page 231. Do charities transfer income to people in poverty? (yes)

4. Read page 233. Is Social Security a government program? (yes)

5. Read page 234. Do welfare programs always help the poor escape poverty? (no)

Intermediate Level Questions

Encourage students at this level to offer verbal responses or short written responses to the following questions.

1. Read page 227. Did the "war" on poverty get rid of poverty in the United States? (No, 12 percent of Americans still live in poverty.)

2. Read page 228. What is the poverty line? (the minimum yearly income that a family must have in order to meet its basic needs)

3. Look at the table on page 228. What was the poverty line for a family of four in 1980? ($8,414)

4. Read page 231. What two groups transfer income to people in poverty? (charities and the government)

5. Read page 233. What government program provides income to people who are retired or unable to work? (the Social Security program)

Advanced Level Questions

Encourage students at this level to provide written responses in complete sentences to the following questions.

1. Why is the poverty line adjusted each year? (Due to inflation, a family needs more money each year to climb out of poverty.)

2. Why is where a person lives an important consideration when measuring a person's standard of living? (The cost of living may vary greatly in different parts of the country.)

3. How do most societies try to deal with poverty? (Most societies try to transfer income from those who have it to those who do not.)

4. How does the Social Security program limit poverty? (The Social Security program provides money to people who are retired or unable to work.)

5. Why have some social welfare programs been attacked in recent years? (Critics claim welfare programs support the poor but do not help them escape poverty.)

▶ Closing the Chapter

Distribute copies of the Spider Web found on page 54 of this guide. Have students label the central topic **Poverty** and the outlying corners **Poverty Line, Standards of Living, Income Transfers,** and **Government Programs.** Then, direct students to use details, terms, and ideas from the chapter to fill in the web. Once webs are completed, have students write a summary of the information that they learned from the chapter.

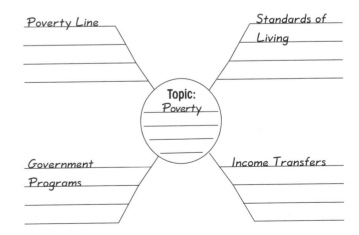

Chapter 19

Government in a Free Market Economy

pages 242–255

▶ Introducing the Chapter

Tapping Prior Knowledge

Ask students to preview the chapter by reading the headings and looking at the photographs, chart, and graph. Then, ask students if they can name some government services that are important to them. For example, ask if they visit museums or local parks, or if they borrow books from a library. Some students might suggest some services they would like the government to offer. Ask students, *Why can the government not always provide the services that people want?*

Preteaching Vocabulary

Personalizing Vocabulary Begin by asking students to preview the chapter for five unfamiliar words or phrases and to record them in their Word Logs. Ask students to use their bilingual dictionaries to define the words or phrases. Students may form small groups to share their Word Logs.

Identifying Essential Vocabulary Go over the pronunciation and meaning of each phrase in the box below. Then, ask students to work with a partner to write the sentence where they find the phrase in the chapter and then to replace the phrase with a familiar word or phrase. Students may wish to consult their bilingual dictionaries as they rewrite the sentences.

Word or Phrase	Meaning
records the sights and sounds	writes down what he sees and hears (p. 243)
no such thing as a free lunch	things that seem free are paid for in some way (p. 248)
vice versa	the other way around; the opposite (p. 251)
take a serious look at	think about changing (p. 251)

▶ Applying Content Knowledge

From the Chapter: You Decide (page 244)

Have students read the You Decide margin note on page 244 of the Student Edition. Then, have them list a government service that they have used recently. Ask them to write a short paragraph explaining why the service is important. As students continue to read the chapter and learn more about the services offered by the government, ask them to add additional services from which they benefit. For each service, ask them to write a short paragraph explaining its importance.

Using Visuals

Ask students to look at the photographs and captions on pages 242 and 245 of the Student Edition. Have the class describe what they see. Point out that both photographs show services offered by the government. Then, ask students to look through magazines and newspapers to find other photographs that show services paid for by the federal, state, or local government. These might include pictures of roads and bridges, the armed services, postal delivery, recreation programs like little league, and national parks. Have students write a caption for each picture they find. Then, have them use the photographs to create a booklet entitled **Government at Work in a Free Market Economy.**

Organizing Information

Distribute copies of the Three-Column Chart found on page 51 of this guide. Have students entitle the chart **Major Taxes** and label the three columns **Name of Tax, What Tax Is Paid On,** and **Who Pays the Tax.** As students read the chapter, ask them to note information about the different major taxes that are described.

Topic: Major Taxes

Name of Tax	What Tax Is Paid On	Who Pays the Tax

Assessing Content Knowledge

Ask students to respond to the following questions. You may wish to encourage students with higher language proficiency to help beginning level students understand the questions.

Beginning Level Questions

Encourage students at this level to think about the answers to these questions and to offer short verbal responses.

1. Look at the photograph and caption on page 242. What are two services provided by the government? (fire and police departments)

2. Read the Words to Know on page 243. Is sales tax or an estate tax a tax on purchases? (sales tax)

3. Look at the photograph and caption on page 245. Are public schools paid for by taxes? (yes)

4. Look at the chart on page 249. How many different types of taxes does it describe? (seven)

5. Look at Graph 19.1 on page 252. What kind of graph is this? (a pie graph or circle graph)

Intermediate Level Questions

Encourage students at this level to offer verbal responses or short written responses to the following questions.

1. Read pages 244 and 245. How many levels of government provide goods and services to its citizens? (three)

2. Read page 246. What economic policy says government should not interfere with business? (laissez faire)

3. Read page 247. Which federal organization studies environmental problems and helps regulate pollution? (the Environmental Protection Agency)

4. Look at the chart on page 249. What tax is charged on the property of someone who has died? (estate tax)

5. Look at Graph 19.1 on page 252. What percentage of total federal taxes are corporate income taxes? (10%)

Advanced Level Questions

Encourage students at this level to provide written responses in complete sentences to the following questions.

1. What are some services that the government provides? (Possible answers: police and fire services, public schools, public parks, military, roads, courts)

2. What do people who believe in laissez faire want? (People who believe in laissez faire believe the government should not interfere with business.)

3. How do governments get the money to pay for goods and services? (Governments pay for goods and services by raising taxes.)

4. Who pays property taxes and who receives them? (Owners of property pay taxes on land and houses to state and local governments.)

5. How can citizens change the role of the government in the economy? (Citizens can elect officials who want the government to play a bigger or smaller role in government.)

Closing the Chapter

Distribute copies of the Who, What, Why, Where, When, and How Chart found on page 61 of this guide. Ask students to copy the following questions onto their charts: **Who pays taxes? What is laissez faire? Why should government regulate economic activity? Where do some important government goods and services go? When should government not get involved?** and **How can citizens change the role of government?** Then, have them answer each question. When the chart is complete, have students use it to summarize the main ideas of the chapter.

WHO	Who pays taxes?
WHAT	What is laissez faire?
WHY	Why should government regulate economic activity?
WHERE	Where do some important government goods and services go?
WHEN	When should government not get involved?
HOW	How can citizens change the role of government?

Chapter 20

Government Budget and National Debt

pages 256–265

Introducing the Chapter

Tapping Prior Knowledge

Have students preview the chapter by reading the headings and by looking at the graph and table. Ask students, *What does it mean to be in debt? Why would most people prefer not to be in debt? What do you do when you want to buy something but you do not have enough money?* Then, have students read the definition of *national debt* in the Words to Know on page 257 of the Student Edition. Determine whether students are aware that the federal government is in debt to its people. Then, ask them to suggest why the federal government might tend to spend more money than it receives in most years.

Preteaching Vocabulary

Personalizing Vocabulary Have students form small groups. Have each group look for ten unfamiliar words or phrases from different sections of the chapter. Once groups have identified these words or phrases, ask them to record the words or phrases in their Word Logs and to use their bilingual dictionaries to define them.

Identifying Essential Vocabulary Go over the pronunciation and meaning of each phrase in the box below. Then, ask students to work with a partner to write the sentence where they find the phrase in the chapter and then to replace the phrase with a familiar word or phrase.

Word or Phrase	Meaning
out of debt	not owing any money (p. 257)
going into debt	borrowing money (p. 258)
an I.O.U.	I owe you; a letter signed by a person who owes money to another (p. 258)
called for an end	tried to stop (p. 260)
a drain on	a loss to (p. 260)
future generations	our children and grandchildren (p. 261)
chief function	main job (p. 262)

Applying Content Knowledge

From the Chapter: You Decide (page 260)

Have students read the You Decide margin note on page 260 of the Student Edition. Discuss an answer to the question as a class. Prompt further discussion with the following question: *How do you feel about paying taxes for the interest on money that was spent years ago?* Then, ask them, *Do you think the government should cut back on its programs in order to pay off some of the national debt? Do you think Americans would be willing to pay higher taxes to pay off the national debt?* Have students summarize the discussion in a short position paper.

Using Visuals

Ask students to redraw the line graph of the national debt shown on page 259 of the Student Edition as a bar graph. Ask them to use the same title and labels that appear on the left side and bottom of the graph. Then, direct them to draw a bar that shows the amount of the debt for each of the years: 1960, 1970, 1980, 1990, and 1998.

Organizing Information

Distribute copies of the Two-Column Chart found on page 50 of this guide. Have students title the chart **The National Debt** and label the two columns **Pros** and **Cons**. As students read about the national debt and its effects on the U.S. economy, ask them to fill in the chart. In the Pros column, students may list the reasons for why the government's deficit may not be harmful. In the Cons column, students may list some of the real and possible drawbacks of having a large national debt. Students may use information from the text as well as prior knowledge.

Using Resources

Invite students to use the Internet and other resources to research whether the federal government has had surpluses or deficits since the year 2000. Have students form groups and share figures to ensure accuracy. Then, have groups show their combined results in a bar graph.

Assessing Content Knowledge

Ask students to respond to the following questions. You may wish to encourage students with higher language proficiency to help beginning level students understand the questions.

Beginning Level Questions

Encourage students at this level to think about the answers to these questions and to offer short verbal responses.

1. Read the Words to Know on page 257. Is a budget surplus or deficit a financial situation in which spending is greater than income or revenues? (a budget deficit)

2. Read the headings on page 258. Does the government have a debt? (yes)

3. Look at Graph 20.1 on page 259. Has the U.S. national debt increased or decreased in recent years? (increased)

4. Read the heading on page 260. True or false: Not everyone agrees on what to do about the national debt. (true)

5. Look at the table on page 261. Which years does the table cover? (1800–1998)

Intermediate Level Questions

Encourage students at this level to offer verbal responses or short written responses to the following questions.

1. Look at the photograph and caption on page 256. How is a photograph of the U.S. Congress relevant to the national debt? (The U.S. Congress debates the budget for the nation.)

2. Read page 258. How does the federal government borrow money? (by selling bonds)

3. Look at Graph 20.1 on page 259. What was the national debt in 1998? (more than 5,500 billion dollars)

4. Read page 260. How might the government pay back the national debt? (by raising taxes)

5. Look at the table on page 261. What was the per capita public debt in the United States in 1990? ($13,000)

Advanced Level Questions

Encourage students at this level to provide written responses in complete sentences to the following questions.

1. How does the federal government develop a budget deficit? (The government develops a deficit by spending more than it receives in taxes or income.)

2. According to Graph 20.1 on page 259, how did the national debt change between 1980 and 1990? (The national debt tripled during these years.)

3. What does the national debt mean for ordinary taxpayers? (More and more of our taxes go to pay the interest on the national debt.)

4. Does the high national debt mean the country may go bankrupt? (No, the country can raise taxes, if necessary, to pay the debt.)

5. Why do you think many Americans are troubled by the growing national debt? (Many Americans think that it is unwise to spend more than your income for long periods of time.)

▶ Closing the Chapter

Distribute copies of the Spider Web found on page 54 of this guide. Ask students to label the central topic **The National Debt** and the outlying corners **Budget Deficits, Government Bonds, Recent Growth of National Debt,** and **Drawbacks of National Debt.** Then, direct students to use details, terms, and ideas from the chapter to fill in the web. Once webs are completed, have students write a summary of the information that they learned from the chapter.

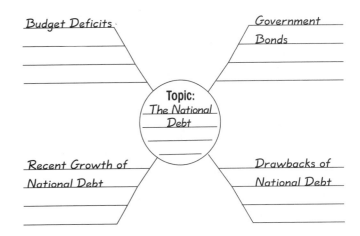

Chapter 21 / Trying to Solve the Economy's Problems

pages 266–277

▶ Introducing the Chapter

Tapping Prior Knowledge

Ask students to think about some of the economic challenges that they face each day (bus money to get around, tickets to a dance, buying lunch, planning for college tuition). Have them state some of the problems that face our country's economy. Remind students, for example, that they have read about inflation, unemployment, and a rising national debt. Then, have students preview the chapter by reading the headings and subheadings. Finally, ask volunteers to suggest how the government might try to improve the country's economy.

Preteaching Vocabulary

Personalizing Vocabulary Have students form small groups. Have each group look for ten unfamiliar words or phrases from different sections of the chapter. Once groups have identified these words or phrases, ask them to record the words or phrases in their Word Logs and to use their bilingual dictionaries to define them. As a class, the groups may share their Word Logs.

Identifying Essential Vocabulary Go over the pronunciation and meaning of each phrase in the box below. Then, ask students to work in pairs to write a sentence for each phrase.

Word or Phrase	Meaning
limit spending	spend less (p. 269)
to be put into effect	to start (p. 269)
to boost	to raise (p. 269)
in its vault	in a bank's safe (p. 271)
taken out of circulation	not able to be used (p. 272)
get to keep more of their money	pay fewer taxes (p. 273)
fine tune	make small changes to solve problems (p. 274)

▶ Applying Content Knowledge

From the Chapter: Great Economic Thinkers: Milton Friedman (page 274)

Ask students to read Great Economic Thinkers: Milton Friedman on page 274 of the Student Edition. Discuss with students all of the things that Milton Friedman believes about fiscal policy and monetary policy. Ask students, *Why do you think Milton Friedman is one of the great economic thinkers of our time?*

Using Manipulatives

Ask students to make a flashcard for each of the Words to Know on page 267 of the Student Edition. Have them write the word or phrase on one side of the card and its definition on the back. Then, after reading each section of the chapter, call on a student to summarize the main ideas of that section, using the Words to Know that appear in dark type in that section.

Organizing Information

Distribute copies of the Main Idea and Supporting Details Chart found on page 58 of this guide. Have students label the main idea box **How the Federal Reserve Controls the Money Supply**. Then, ask students to read pages 270–272 of the Student Edition. Ask them to fill the supporting details boxes with information about how the money supply is controlled. For example, students should list reserves, interest rates, and government bonds and include information about each of them. Finally, students should write a conclusion of the process in the summary box.

Summarizing

Ask students to work in pairs to read and answer the Check Your Understanding questions on pages 269, 270, and 272 of the Student Edition. Suggest that students alternate reading and answering the questions. Have students use their answers to write two or more paragraphs that summarize the chapter. Students may use their summaries to review Chapter 21 of the Student Edition.

Assessing Content Knowledge

Ask students to respond to the following questions. You may wish to encourage students with higher language proficiency to help beginning level students understand the questions.

Beginning Level Questions

Encourage students at this level to think about the answers to these questions and to offer short verbal responses.

1. Look at the photograph and caption on page 266. What government program created thousands of jobs during the Great Depression? (the WPA)

2. Read the Words to Know on page 267. True or false: The prime rate is the lowest interest rate that banks offer their best business customers. (true)

3. Read the headings on pages 268 and 270. What are two economic policies? (fiscal policy and monetary policy)

4. Read pages 271 and 272. How many ways does the Federal Reserve control the money supply? (three)

5. Read the heading on page 273. What economic theory was tried in the 1980s? (supply-side economics)

Intermediate Level Questions

Encourage students at this level to offer verbal responses or short written responses to the following questions.

1. Read page 268. Would the federal government raise or lower spending to cut unemployment? (raise spending)

2. Read pages 268 and 269. Why might government cut spending and raise taxes? (to control inflation)

3. Read page 270. Why might the government increase the money supply? (to fight high unemployment)

4. Read pages 271 and 272. What are the three ways in which the Federal Reserve encourages or discourages bank loans? (by setting the reserve requirement, by changing the discount rate, and by buying and selling government bonds)

5. Read page 273. What economic theory says producing more goods and services is the best way to fight unemployment and inflation? (supply-side economics)

Advanced Level Questions

Encourage students at this level to provide written responses in complete sentences to the following questions.

1. How might government use fiscal policy to control inflation? (The government might cut spending or raise taxes to fight inflation.)

2. What argument do some economists use against fiscal policy? (Changes in taxes and government spending take too long to work; it isn't clear if they work at all.)

3. How might the government use monetary policy to fight high unemployment? (The government might increase the money supply.)

4. How does the Federal Reserve increase the money supply? (The Federal Reserve encourages banks to make more loans.)

5. What do supply-side economists believe about taxes and government? (They believe taxes should be cut and the size of government should be decreased.)

Closing the Chapter

Distribute copies of the Outline found on page 55 of this guide. Ask students to label the outline **How the Government Solves Economic Problems.** Then, have them use the information from the chapter to complete the outline. After the outline is completed, have students use it to summarize the main ideas of the chapter.

Topic: How the Government Solves Economic Problems
I. Fiscal Policy and Monetary Policy
   A. How Fiscal Policy Can Help
      1. _____
      2. _____
   B. How Monetary Policy Can Help
      1. _____
      2. _____
II. How the Federal Reserve Increases Money Supply
   A. Reserves
      1. _____
      2. _____
   B. Interest Rates
      1. _____
      2. _____
   C. Government Bonds
      1. _____
      2. _____

Chapter 22 / International Trade

pages 280–291

▶ Introducing the Chapter

Tapping Prior Knowledge

Have students preview the chapter by reading the headings and looking at the photographs. Ask students, *What are some goods that you buy or use that come from countries other than the United States?* Students might name cars made in Japan, fruits and vegetables grown in Latin America, or clothing and toys made in China. Then, ask students, *What are some products made in the United States that are popular in other countries?* Students might list movies, blue jeans, and music CDs. Point out that the title of the chapter is "International Trade" and that *international* means "between nations." Based on this discussion, have students make predictions about what they might learn in the chapter.

Preteaching Vocabulary

Personalizing Vocabulary Have students form small groups. Have each group look for ten unfamiliar words or phrases from different sections of the chapter. Once groups have identified these words or phrases, ask them to record the words or phrases in their Word Logs and to use their bilingual dictionaries to define them. As a class, the groups may share their Word Logs.

Identifying Essential Vocabulary Go over the pronunciation and meaning of each word or phrase in the box below. Then, ask students to work with a partner to write the sentence where they find the word or phrase in the chapter and then to replace the word or phrase with a familiar word or phrase.

Word or Phrase	Meaning
on the other hand	alternately (p. 286)
buy American	buy goods made in the United States (p. 286)
skyrocketed	rose rapidly (p. 287)
most evident results	most obvious results (p. 287)
centered around	was mainly about (p. 288)

▶ Applying Content Knowledge

From the Chapter: Photographs (pages 280 and 282)

Ask students to look at the photographs and captions on pages 280 and 282 of the Student Edition. Discuss with students the types of goods that are being imported to the United States in the photographs. Then, ask students to find magazine or newspaper photographs of other products that the United States is likely to import or export. Have students create a poster of their photographs. One side of the poster should show products that are imported and the other side should display exports. Students may wish to consult an almanac for information on U.S. trade. Display finished posters in the classroom.

Personalizing the Lesson

Show students the label on a shirt that tells where the shirt was made. Ask students to look closely at the labels of some of the clothing, toys, foods, and other products they and their families use. Ask students to make a list of such products and where they were made. Then, have students draw conclusions about the types of goods that the United States imports in a short summary.

Role-Playing

Invite pairs of students to role-play an argument between two economists. One economist believes in free trade. The other is a protectionist. Ask students to use details on pages 285–288 of the Student Edition to find points each would try to make in the argument.

Organizing Information

Distribute copies of the Two-Column Chart found on page 50 of this guide. Have students entitle the chart **Free Trade: Advantages and Disadvantages** and label the two columns **Pros of Free Trade** and **Cons of Free Trade**. Then, as students read pages 285–288 of the Student Edition, ask them to list some advantages and disadvantages of free trade and agreements such as NAFTA.

Assessing Content Knowledge

Ask students to respond to the following questions. You may wish to encourage students with higher language proficiency to help beginning level students understand the questions.

Beginning Level Questions

Encourage students at this level to think about the answers to these questions and to offer short verbal responses.

1. Look at the photograph and caption on page 280. Does better transportation increase trade? (yes)

2. Look at the Words to Know on page 281. Is an import or an export a good sold to another country? (export)

3. Read page 283. Does international trade let countries specialize in producing certain goods? (yes)

4. Read page 286. What is a tax on imports called? (a tariff)

5. Read page 287. What agreement will lead to free trade between the United States, Canada, and Mexico? (NAFTA)

Intermediate Level Questions

Encourage students at this level to offer verbal responses or short written responses to the following questions.

1. Read the Words to Know on page 281. What is protectionism? (the policy of limiting trade with other countries to protect domestic industries)

2. Read page 283. Why do countries specialize in producing certain goods? (Different countries have different resources and opportunity costs.)

3. Read page 284. Does the United States have a trade surplus or a trade deficit with some of its trading partners? (trade deficit)

4. Read pages 285 and 286. What is the opposite of protectionism? (free trade)

5. Look at the chart on page 289. How many Austrian schillings does $1 U.S. equal? (11.89 schillings)

Advanced Level Questions

Encourage students at this level to provide written responses in complete sentences to the following questions.

1. How does international trade and specialization improve the lives of consumers? (Consumers get to buy better products at lower prices than they would if there was no international trade.)

2. How would a country develop a trade surplus? (If the value of a country's exports is more than the value of the country's imports, the country would have a trade surplus.)

3. Why might the U.S. government place a protective tariff on imported automobiles? (The tariff would increase the price of imported cars. Consumers might then buy more American cars and jobs in the auto industry would be saved.)

4. How do people who support NAFTA think it will help the United States? (Supporters of NAFTA say the agreement will make it easier for the United States to export goods. This will create more jobs in the United States.)

5. How is the exchange rate for currencies of different countries set? (The supply of and demand for different currencies set the exchange rate.)

▶ Closing the Chapter

Distribute copies of the Two-Column Chart found on page 50 of this guide. Ask students to entitle the chart **International Trade** and label the two columns **Cause** and **Effect.** In the Effect column, dictate the following list to students: *a country specializes in making certain products, a country develops a trade surplus, a country develops a trade deficit, a country imposes a trade tariff,* and *a country calls for an embargo.* Then, have students write a few sentences that give a likely cause for each of these effects. After the chart is completed, have students use it to summarize the main ideas of the chapter.

Topic: International Trade

Cause	Effect

Chapter 23 Developing Countries pages 292–305

▶ Introducing the Chapter

Tapping Prior Knowledge
Ask students to preview the chapter by reading the headings and subheadings. Then, have students look at the photograph and caption on page 292 of the Student Edition. Ask students, *How might the lives of the people living in the mud huts be different from the lives of the people living in the modern apartments?* Based on this discussion, have students make predictions about what they will learn.

Preteaching Vocabulary
Personalizing Vocabulary Have students form small groups. Have each group look for ten unfamiliar words or phrases from different sections of the chapter. Once groups have identified these words or phrases, ask them to record the words or phrases in their Word Logs and to use their bilingual dictionaries to define them. As a class, the groups may share their Word Logs.

Identifying Essential Vocabulary Go over the pronunciation and meaning of each word or phrase in the box below. Next, distribute an index card to each student. Ask students to write a question on the index card using one or more of the vocabulary terms. Then, have students exchange cards with a partner and answer their partner's question.

Word or Phrase	Meaning
standing almost in the shadows of	very close to (p. 293)
a better life awaits	the future will be better (p. 294)
loom over	are high above (p. 294)
bustling	very busy (p. 295)
know-how	knowledge and skills (p. 297)
most populous	having the most people (p. 297)
a moral responsibility	wanting to do the right thing (p. 298)
growing pains	problems caused during times of growth (p. 300)

▶ Applying Content Knowledge

From the Chapter: Economics Facts (pages 295, 297, 298, and 299)
Have students read the Economics Facts on pages 295, 297, 298, and 299 of the Student Edition. Ask them to identify and discuss some developing countries with which they are familiar. Tell them to choose one developing country and to conduct additional research on it. Students may conduct research in the library or on the Internet. Then, have students create their own Economics Fact about that country. Facts should list things such as the country's industries, standard of living, literacy rate, and population growth.

Personalizing the Lesson
Tell students to suppose that they are reporters visiting a developing country. They are working on a documentary. The documentary is about the developing country. Have students write a journal entry that describes what the country is like. Have students note family incomes, health, literacy rates, and size. Then, have students compare the overall standard of living of the developing country to the standard of living in the United States. Ask volunteers to read their finished journal entries aloud to the class.

Organizing Information
Have students turn the four section headings of the chapter into questions: *What are two kinds of countries? What are some characteristics of developing countries? How does the world try to face the challenge of helping nations develop?* and *What is the best way for developing nations to overcome their growing pains?* Ask students to copy each question onto a sheet of paper. Then, have them answer the questions. Finally, have students use their answers to write a summary of the main ideas of the chapter.

Assessing Content Knowledge

Ask students to respond to the following questions. You may wish to encourage students with higher language proficiency to help beginning level students understand the questions.

Beginning Level Questions

Encourage students at this level to think about the answers to these questions and to offer short verbal responses.

1. Look at the photograph on page 292. What developing country is shown? (India)
2. Read the Words to Know on page 293. Does a developing country depend mainly on agriculture? (yes)
3. Read pages 294 and 295. Are Japan, Canada, and the United States developing countries? (no)
4. Read the third characteristic on page 296. Do developing countries have a high or low rate of literacy? (low)
5. Read page 298. Who gives foreign aid to developing countries? (developed countries)

Intermediate Level Questions

Encourage students at this level to offer verbal responses or short written responses to the following questions.

1. Look at the Words to Know on page 293. How is a developed country different from a developing country? (A developed country is highly industrialized and has a higher standard of living than a developing country does.)
2. Look at the list of characteristics of developing countries on pages 296 and 297. What are two characteristics of a developing country? (Possible answers: Developing countries usually have a low GDP per person, agricultural economies, a low rate of literacy, poor health conditions, and fast-growing populations.)
3. Read page 296. What is per capita GDP? (a country's gross domestic product divided by the number of people in the population)
4. Read page 299. Who supplies foreign aid to developing nations? (the governments of developed nations and the United Nations)
5. Read page 302. What international organization tries to help developing nations? (the United Nations)

Advanced Level Questions

Encourage students at this level to provide written responses in complete sentences to the following questions.

1. How does the standard of living in developing countries contrast with that in developed countries? (The standard of living is much lower in developing countries.)
2. Why is the life expectancy low in developing countries? (In developing countries, there are few doctors and hospitals, and health care is hard to get.)
3. How will U.S. businesses benefit if developing countries industrialize? (As developing countries industrialize, they will be able to buy more from U.S. businesses.)
4. What are some forms that foreign aid may take? (Possible answers: money, food, capital equipment, military assistance)
5. Why should developing nations try to develop many different industries, not just one? (If a country has many different industries, it will not be dependent on just one product, whose price may fall.)

Closing the Chapter

Distribute copies of Three-Column Chart found on page 51 of this guide. Have students entitle the chart **Comparing Nation Development**. Then, have students label the columns **Factors**, **Developing Nations**, and **Developed Nations**. Tell students to list the categories in the first column as shown on the chart below. Then, as students read the chapter, have them add ideas and details that compare developing nations with developed nations.

Topic: Comparing Nation Development

Factors	Developing Nations	Developed Nations
Industries		
Standard of living		
Literacy		
Life expectancy/ infant mortality		
Population growth		

About the Graphic Organizers

The graphic organizers and visuals provided here can be used in a variety of ways. They can be made into overhead slides and used for visual instruction or for group work. The pages can also be reproduced for use by students. Below is a description of each graphic organizer and visual with suggestions for their use. Each of these graphic organizers can also be downloaded from www.esl-ell.com.

Two-Column Chart (page 50)

This graphic organizer can be used for many purposes. The columns can be labeled as needed. Then, relevant information is written in each column of the chart.

Three-Column Chart (page 51)

This graphic organizer can be used for many purposes. The columns can be labeled as needed. Then, relevant information is written in each column of the chart.

Four-Column Chart (page 52)

This graphic organizer can be used for many purposes. The columns can be labeled as needed. Then, relevant information is written in each column of the chart.

Sequence of Events Chart (page 53)

This graphic organizer is a flowchart that helps students sort information chronologically. You may wish to have students use this graphic organizer when making to-do lists and writing out directions. Students might also use the Sequence of Events Chart to plan out role-playing activities or while writing conversations.

Spider Web (page 54)

This graphic organizer is used to organize several levels of elaboration. The main topic is written in the center circle. Attributes and specific details are listed on the horizontal lines at the corner of the web. This organizer can also be used to determine main ideas and supporting details. You may also want students to use a spider web when brainstorming ideas.

Outline (page 55)

This graphic organizer is used to help students organize and write outlines. An outline can be used to help write paragraphs with fully developed ideas in which supporting details are given. For activities that require longer outlines, extend them by continuing the numbering on the back of the reproducible page.

Idea Web (page 56)

This graphic organizer is used to cluster supporting details around a central topic. It is very useful for brainstorming. The main concept or idea is written in the center shape. Related ideas are listed in the outer shapes.

Venn Diagram (page 57)

This graphic organizer is used to compare and contrast things or ideas. Each circle should be labeled as one of the two things being compared and contrasted. Then, the differences are written in the outer section of each circle. The similarities are written in the section in which the circles overlap.

Main Idea and Supporting Details Chart (page 58)

This graphic organizer is used to identify supporting details that relate to a central topic. The main idea is written in the first box. Supporting details are written in the boxes labeled Supporting Details. Students can use the main idea and supporting details to write a paragraph in the box labeled Summary.

KWL Chart (page 59)

This chart can be used to help students access their knowledge of a topic and to add to what they already know. *K* stands for "what I know." *W* stands for "what I want to know." *L* stands for "what I have learned."

Cause-and-Effect Chart (page 60)

This graphic organizer helps students organize the effects of a particular cause. Students write the cause in the top oval and the effects in the remaining ovals.

Who, What, Why, Where, When, and How Chart (page 61)

This graphic organizer is used to help students identify important information while they read. Students complete the chart by answering the questions as they read. This chart can be used to help students understand textbook chapters or news articles they read.

Problem-Solution Journal (page 62)

This graphic organizer helps students organize problems and their solutions. Students write the problem in the boxes under Problem and the solutions in the boxes under Solution.

Timeline (page 63)

This graphic organizer is used to organize a series of events.

World Map (page 64)

This map allows students to see all the continents at once. It can be used for labeling and identifying activities.

Individual Activity Rubric (page 65)

The Individual Activity Rubric can be customized for different activities. The first eight criteria in the rubric are generic. The last two criteria are left blank. These criteria should be based on specific tasks required and filled in by the teacher. You may wish to distribute a rubric to students as a guide for completing an activity or as a self-assessment tool.

Lesson Planner (page 66)

This worksheet is designed to help teachers create a well-organized lesson. It includes places to list the lesson's objectives, the materials needed, opening and closing activities, as well as any accommodations for students with individual needs.

Chapter Goals and Self-Assessment (page 67)

This reproducible can be used for goal setting and self-assessment. When starting a chapter, have students write the Learning Objectives on this worksheet. At the end of the chapter, students can self-check their understanding by writing about what they learned.

Name _____ Date _____

Two-Column Chart

Topic: _____

Name _____ Date _____

Three-Column Chart

Topic: _____

Name _____ Date _____

Four-Column Chart

Topic: _____

Name _____ Date _____

Sequence of Events Chart

TOPIC

SEQUENCE OF EVENTS

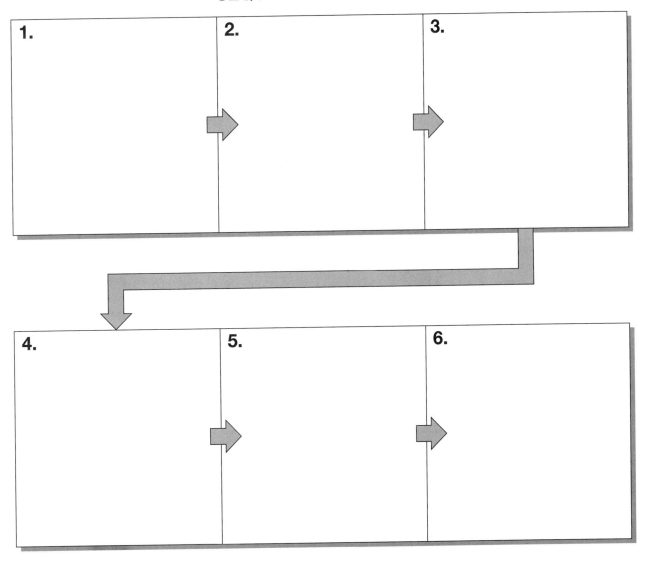

Name _____ Date _____

Spider Web

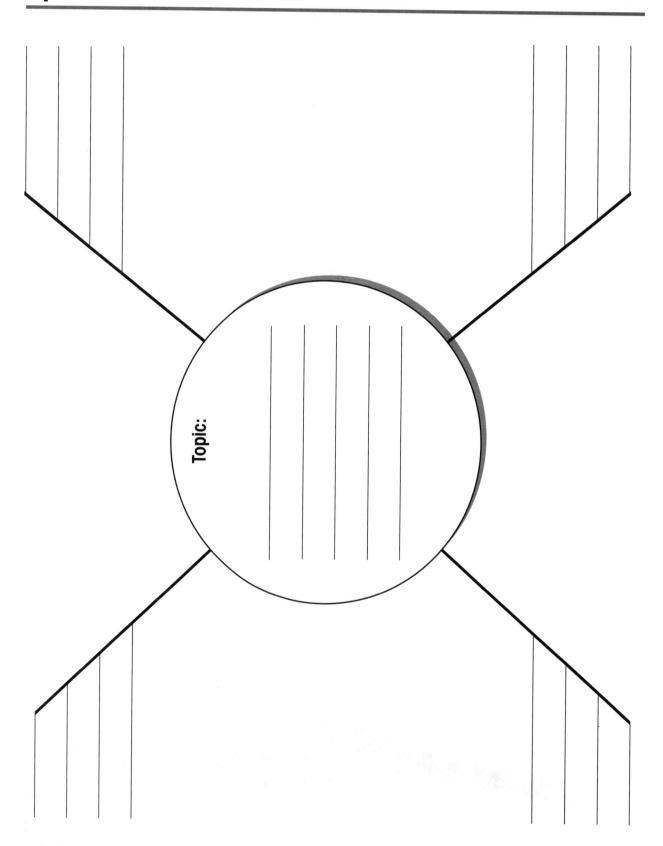

Topic:

Name _____ Date _____

Outline

Topic: _____

I.

   A. _____

     1. _____

     2. _____

   B. _____

     1. _____

     2. _____

   C. _____

     1. _____

     2. _____

II.

   A. _____

     1. _____

     2. _____

   B. _____

     1. _____

     2. _____

   C. _____

     1. _____

     2. _____

Name _____ Date _____

Idea Web

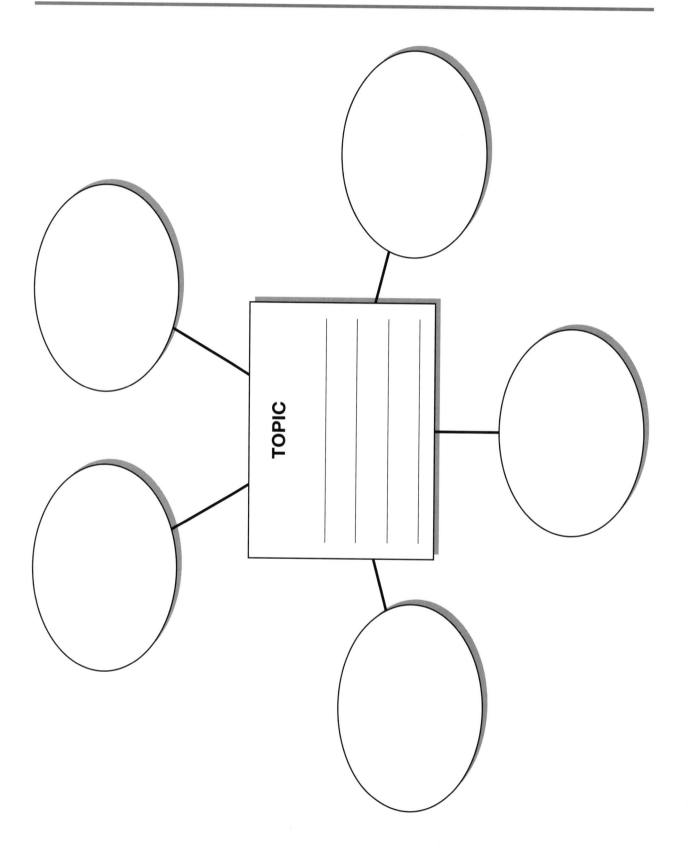

TOPIC

Name _____ Date _____

Venn Diagram

Topic: _____

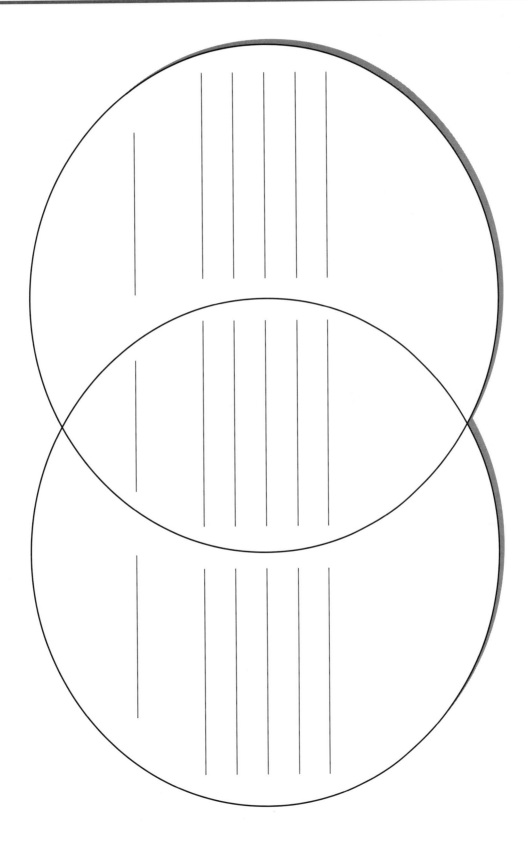

Name _____ Date _____

Main Idea and Supporting Details Chart

MAIN IDEA

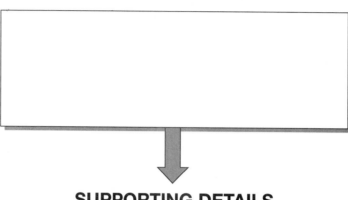

SUPPORTING DETAILS

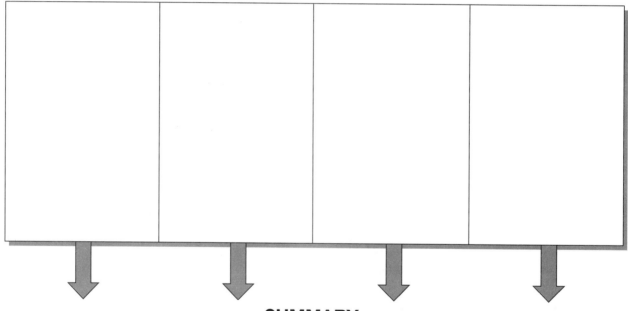

SUMMARY

Name _____ Date _____

KWL Chart

Topic: _____

K (What I Know)	W (What I Want to Know)	L (What I Have Learned)

Name _____ Date _____

Cause-and-Effect Chart

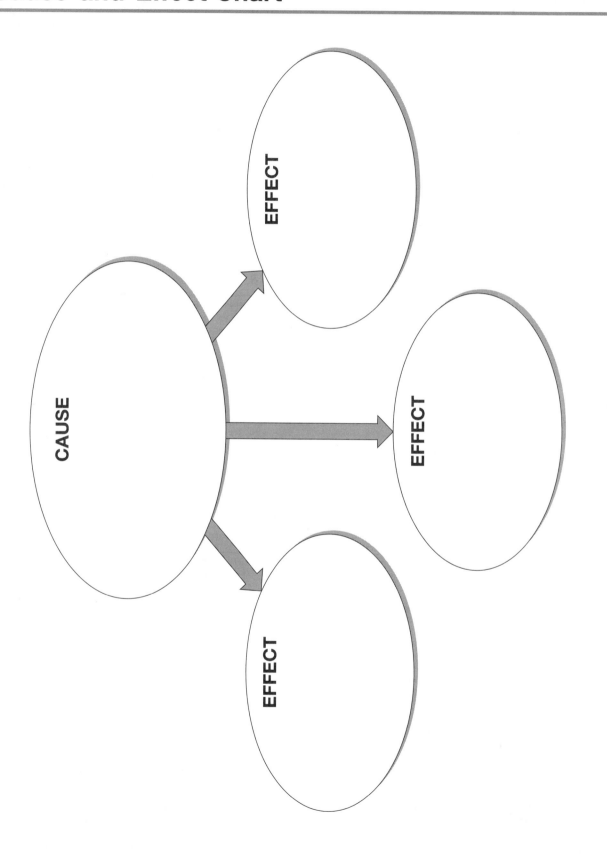

Name _____ Date _____

Who, What, Why, Where, When, and How Chart

WHO	
WHAT	
WHY	
WHERE	
WHEN	
HOW	

Name _____ Date _____

Problem-Solution Journal

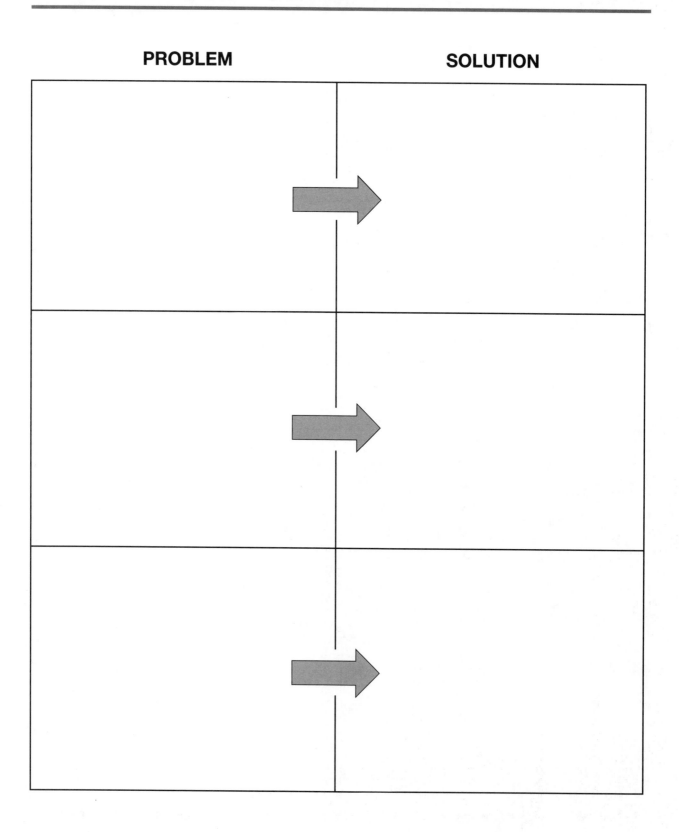

PROBLEM   **SOLUTION**

Name _____ Date _____

Timeline

Name _____ Date _____

World Map

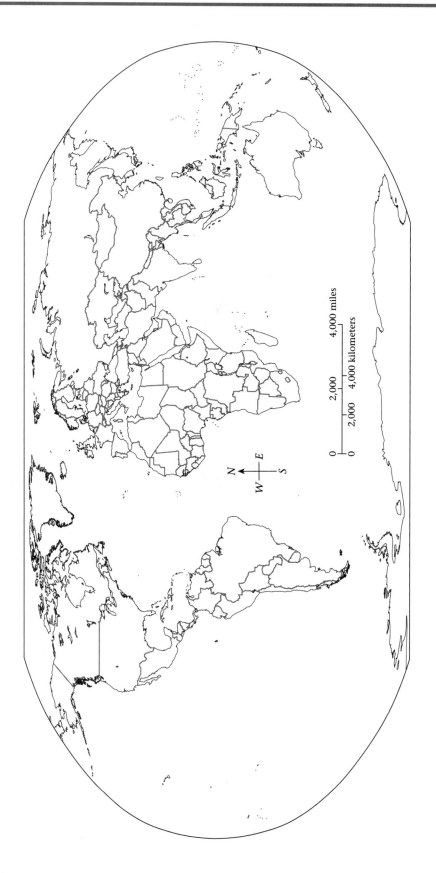

Individual Activity Rubric

Name _____ Date _____

Chapter Number _____ Activity _____

Directions
Check ✓ one box in a column to finish each sentence.
Give each check ✓ the assigned number of points.
Add the points in each column. Write the sum. Then, add across to find
the total score. You may wish to add two criteria of your own to the rubric.

POINTS	10	9	8	7	6
For this activity, [student's name]_____	all of the time	most of the time	half of the time	less than half of the time	none of the time
followed directions					
asked questions when help was needed					
worked independently when required					
used appropriate resources and materials					
completed assigned tasks					
showed an understanding of the content					
presented materials without errors					
explained thinking with support					
_____					
_____					
POINTS	+	+	+	+	=

TOTAL SCORE

Lesson Planner

Name _____ Date _____

Class _____ Chapter _____

Objective(s) _____
_____

Materials _____
_____

Resources	Student Edition	Teacher's Answer Edition	Workbook	Classroom Resource Binder

Teaching Plan

❑ Open _____
_____

❑ Teach _____
_____

❑ Close _____
_____

❑ Assignment _____
_____

❑ Assessment _____
_____

Mixed Abilities

❑ Reteaching _____
_____

❑ Reinforcement _____
_____

❑ Enrichment _____
_____

Individual Needs

❑ ESL/ELL _____
_____

❑ Learning Styles _____
_____

Chapter Goals and Self-Assessment

Name _____ Date _____

Chapter Number _____ Activity _____

Write each Learning Objective on a line below.   **Did I understand it?**

                                                              Yes   No

- _____   ❏   ❏

- _____   ❏   ❏

- _____   ❏   ❏

- _____   ❏   ❏

- _____   ❏   ❏

- _____   ❏   ❏

Complete each statement.

This chapter is about _____

_____.

An important economic concept from this chapter is _____

_____.

I also learned about some other economic concepts. One of them is _____

_____.

I completed Chapter _____ entitled _____

_____ and all of my Learning Objectives on

_____.